This 2006 edition published by Barnes & Noble, Inc.
by arrangement with Carlton Books.

editorial manager: Venetia Penfold
editor: Zia Mattocks
art director: Penny Stock
senior art editor: Barbara Zuñiga
special photography: Graham Atkins-Hughes
stylist: Emily Jewsbury
hair & makeup: Debbie Korrie at Michaeljohn
location research: *Prudence Korda*
production: Janette Davis

ISBN-10: 0-7607-8703-4
ISBN-13: 978-0-7607-8703-8

CIP data is available from the Library of Congress.

Printed and bound in Dubai

1 3 5 7 9 10 8 6 4 2

The author, publisher and licensor have made every effort to ensure that all information on the use of essential oils is correct and up to date at the time of publication. However, the application and quality of essential oils is beyond the control of the above parties, who cannot be held responsible for any problems resulting from their use. Do not use essential oils without prior consultation with a qualified aromatherapist if you are pregnant, taking any form of medication, or if you suffer from oversensitive skin. Half-doses should be used for children and the elderly.

home spa

pamper yourself
from head to toe

Chrissie Painell-Malkin

BARNES & NOBLE
NEW YORK

contents

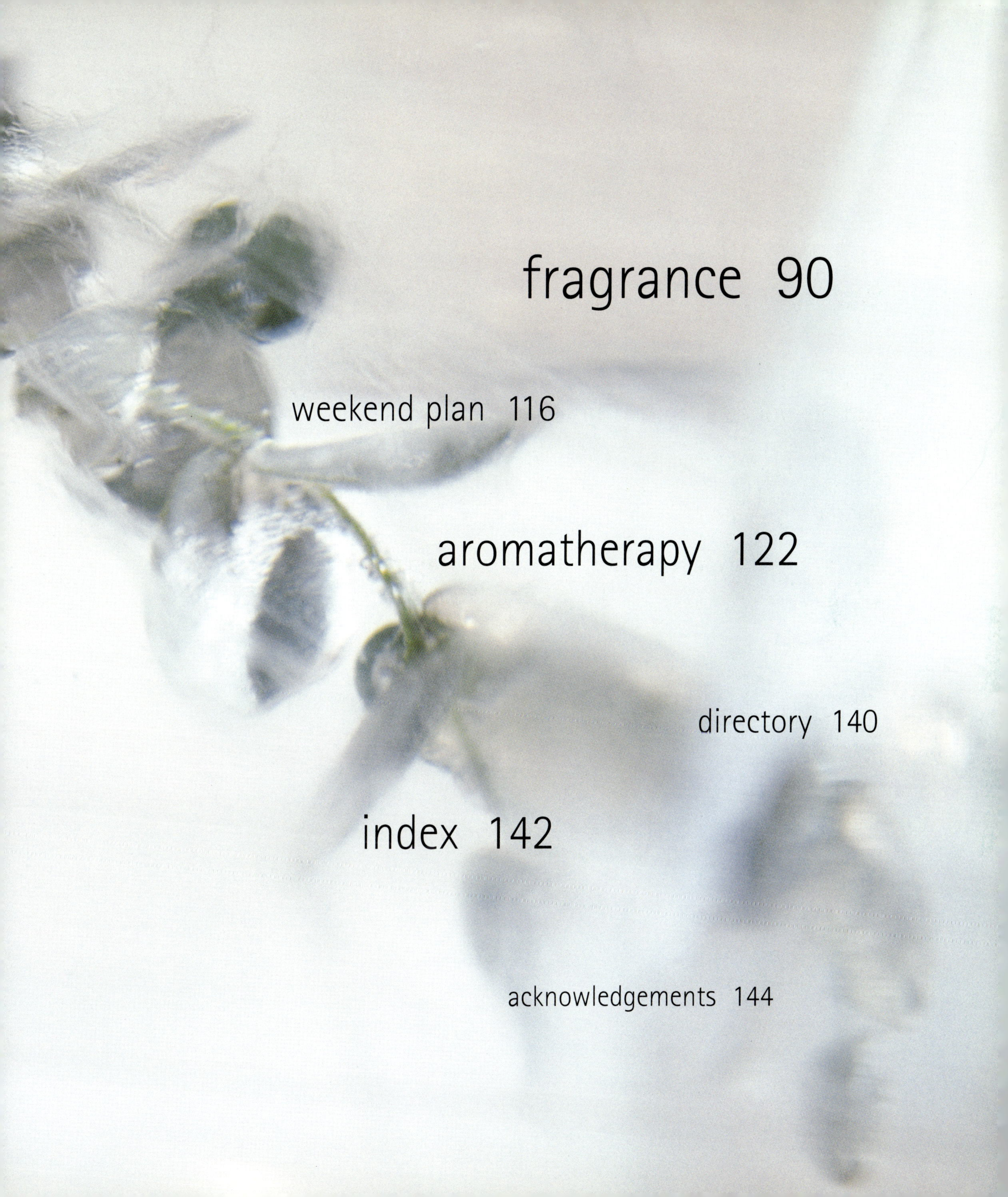

pamper yourself from head to toe

The home is now considered the place to be. It's where we can close the door on the world and enter our personal comfort zone. *Home Spa* explains how to bring some of the professional beauty therapy and spa experiences into your own home with luxurious, holistic treatments designed to pamper the body, mind and spirit.

Nature has given us a wealth of herbs, plants and flowers that can make a real difference to our physical and emotional wellbeing. *Home Spa* taps into the power of these healing and restorative botanical ingredients to show you how to feel truly fabulous in the minimum of time. There are easy-to-follow essential oil-based recipes that will help to restore your energy and revitalize your skin and hair. Facials, massages, herbal and aromatherapy baths, make-up techniques and fragrances are all featured in this practical and inspirational guide.

Time often plays a deciding role in how well we look after ourselves, and women are notoriously good at putting everyone else first and notoriously bad at considering themselves. However, the only way you are going to find the time to exercise, to prepare fresh foods and – if you are really lucky – to escape for the occasional facial, massage or complementary health treatment is by giving yourself high priority. To be able to find the energy and enthusiasm for family, friends, work, sport and creativity, you need to establish a balance.

Equilibrium comes from having the optimum amount of mental stimulation and physical relaxation – a challenging job or pastime and a fulfilling social life. We shouldn't forget, though, that we need to have time to listen to our souls.

Do whatever it takes to stay in touch with your needs right now – reshuffle your routine to allow more time for yourself. Learn to meditate, and incorporate natural healing treatments like aromatherapy, reflexology and massage into your schedule. Recognize that rest and relaxation are your right, not just everyone else's.

Home Spa is a down-to-earth guide to taking more care of yourself in an increasingly demanding world, using the ingredients provided by nature.

In *Home Spa*, learn how to maximize your bath time to revive your spirits and reconnect your body to your mind. The process of polishing your skin with a beautifully scented scrub, and then moisturizing top to toe until you are satin-smooth, does a lot more than simply improve the condition of your skin. It is part of the process of transformation that health and beauty rituals are all about. We are telling ourselves subconsciously that we are worth all of this self-love, attention and time. It is the action of self-healing. The great bonus is that by adding essential oils to our bath and bodycare programmes we can tune into our psyche and help our physical systems to rebalance themselves.

Look afresh at skincare, focusing on how the skin changes from day to day. By recognizing that our skin's requirements are not restricted to those of our inherited skin type, we can give our complexions and bodies the right treatments at the right times. Recent research has found that applying vitamins to the surface of the skin can reduce the appearance of fine lines and wrinkles by improving the skin's supportive collagen and elastin network. This was found to have a much greater effect on the skin's condition than taking supplements orally. Essential oils have protective, anti-ageing and regenerative properties when applied to the skin. The carrier oils in which they need to be diluted before application are rich in vitamins that are important to the skin's metabolism. When you apply a face mask or a moisturizer that contains essential oils, or massage the face and body with these potent essences, you are undoubtedly giving yourself a helping hand in the struggle against ageing.

Hair often demands constant attention, but using the right haircare products and tools will help you control and maintain your hair type and style.

Super-natural is the key when it comes to no-fuss make-up, and *Home Spa* explains how sheer textures and a light touch are the basis for a fresh-faced look.

Fragrance is one of life's great pleasures. A special scent has the ability to trigger the most powerful memories and emotions. You can infuse different fragrances to enhance your environment – scents that will make guests feel welcome, aromas to help you concentrate when you're working, and signature scents that will underscore your personality.

Aromatherapy is the science of using essential oils to help re-energize the body and mind. From camomile to clary sage, lavender to lemon, discover the properties of key oils and how best to use them safely.

Whenever you're in need of a pick-me-up, turn to the Weekend Plan (page 116). You will learn how to pamper yourself with abandon, and the tricks you discover can be easily incorporated into your everyday beauty routine.

If you love beauty products and the whole ritual of being a woman, you will find lots to inform and excite you. Enjoy!

bathing & bodycare

Whether your aim is to cleanse, refresh, purify or soak, bathing can be a sensory and therapeutic experience ... Awaken your senses with an invigorating shower or relax in an aromatic bath. Wrap yourself in your softest towel and slather your body with hydrating moisturizer, silky-smooth, perfumed oil or a rejuvenating splash to leave yourself feeling truly pampered.

'She lowered herself into the warm bath and lay up to her breasts in water made smooth with oil of lavender and pine. Trailing her arms along the sides of the bath, she stroked the roll top with the palm of her hands. How reassuring old enamel was ... for an hour she lay there, between dream and waking, turning the warm tap with her toe whenever the water cooled.'

Roger Housden, *Soul and Sensuality*

Far more than simply being the room in which you wash yourself, the bathroom is the ultimate sanctuary – a place where you can pamper yourself, blissfully cocooned away from the crazy rush of the world outside.

Bathing can be pure hedonism, with its ritualistic pleasures of creamy soaps, exfoliating sponges, nourishing oils and therapeutic essences. Soaking in a hot, fragranced bath may be one of the few chances you have to indulge in private time. It stills the mind, and then allows you to dream a little. How many of us make our grandest plans lying in our bathtubs?

Water has been called the greatest of all healers and throughout history it has been used for religious purification. Today, washing is still very much associated with a renewed sense of self. We bathe to rinse away our stress and tension, and to cleanse the mind, body and spirit of negative feelings and emotions. Some experts believe that we find suspending ourselves in water so therapeutic because it returns us to our prehistoric past when we were all creatures of the sea, as well as returning us to the womb.

Your bathroom is very much a testament to your individual taste and style. If you are a minimalist, it may be an urban, creamy marble haven, with chic mirrored cabinets and inviting, concealed lighting. A pure romantic may prefer a vibrant Mediterranean-style setting, with richly hued handmade tiles, aqua-blue painted walls and a huge freestanding bath.

Interior designers employ canny techniques to ensure that contemporary domestic bathrooms are every bit as luxurious as those found in the finest hotels. Some of these principles can be adopted on a small scale at home to help you create a comfortable, peaceful bathtime setting.

a tranquil haven

Invest in a heated towel rail and the fluffiest towels, softest robe and cosiest slippers you can find.

Always make sure that the room is warm before you take your bath. Purists who want the sensuality of wood or tiles under their feet do not have to compromise on comfort – you can always rip up the bathroom floor and install underfloor heating!

Buy an extra-large shower head and have it fitted into the ceiling directly above your head (unless the ceiling is very high, in which case the water may cool too much before it reaches you).

Decorate the room with beautifully designed fittings and finishes. Enamelled glass panelling is available that can be used instead of tiles on the floor and walls. Both mirrors and glass reflect light and create an illusion of space.

Tidy as much unsightly clutter away as possible and then make a feature of exquisitely designed bodycare products – jars of natural soaps, rows of simple glass bottles and utilitarian metal tins of bath salts. Chrome or plastic holders are aesthetically pleasing and convenient to use in a modern bathroom, while wicker baskets serve the same purpose in a more traditional setting.

Light scented candles to delight the senses and instil an aura of calm. Citrus scents like lemon and orange are uplifting; lavender and rose are calming; and marine notes are reminiscent of ocean breezes. These fragrances will restore your spirits and transport your mind to the peaceful countryside or a tropical island.

Keep a battery-operated CD player or tape-deck nearby and play your favourite soothing music. Some relaxing soundtracks feature recordings of the sea, tropical birds, the calls of whales or dolphins, or age-old chants and mantras that will speak to your soul.

the home spa bath

All of the mind and body treats that you incorporate into your bathing routine will restore your vitality and calm your mind, as well as reinvigorate your body, soften and fragrance your skin and leave you feeling truly pampered. Whichever accessories and products you use, both during your bath and after it – from the body brush, exfoliating mitt or sponge to the aromatic foam bath, scented scrub and perfumed body milk – they will contribute to the sensual experience of bathing. The added benefit is that if you include essential oils in your routine, their healing qualities will further enhance the restorative and harmonizing process. Whether you need to wake yourself up in the morning with an invigorating hot shower or wallow in a fragrant bath by the light of a scented candle, treat your bathtime as a pleasure and a luxury.

skin brushing

Skin brushing improves both circulation and lymph drainage, and also assists in eliminating toxins from the surface of the skin. The lymphatic system is the body's way of disposing of waste and toxins. Lymph does not have a pump to drive it around the body. Instead, it is powered by the movement of the muscles and can also be stimulated by brushing the skin. This technique is increasingly being incorporated into spa treatments worldwide, where beauty therapists and practitioners of complementary medicine may offer to demonstrate it to you.

Using a brush with natural bristles, brush your dry skin once a day before you step into the bath or shower. Start on the soles of your feet and work upwards, always brushing towards your heart to encourage the blood to flow in this direction. You will probably be surprised at how briskly a beauty therapist brushes your body – initially it could take your breath away. Brush yourself as firmly as feels comfortable; after a few days your skin will become accustomed to the sensation and you will be able to increase the pressure a little. If you wish, you can very gently brush your face as well as your body.

Wash the brush regularly in warm soapy water and hang it up to allow it to dry. (Avoid skin brushing if you are unwell, if you have a skin disorder or very sensitive skin.)

skin buffers

You can also stimulate the circulation and exfoliate dead skin cells by using a mitt or friction strap on moist skin when you are in the bath or shower. These skin-smoothers are made of horsehair and sisal fibres and are very hard-wearing. Use either long, sweeping strokes or small, circular movements – and don't apply too much pressure. Mitts and small round loofahs are also available for use on the face, although these buffers are not recommended for anyone with sensitive skin.

sponges

Natural sponges provide a gentle, soothing way of cleansing the skin. Ideally, they should be ecologically harvested from the ocean, washed in sea water, soaked to remove any impurities, then cleaned and dried in the sun. They are suitable for all skin types, including children's.

scrubs

To give your skin an extra, energizing tingle, slough away the surface layer of dead cells that make your skin look dull using a moisturizing foaming scrub that contains plant micro-particles and essential oils such as mood-boosting and skin-toning ylang ylang and lavender. Apply it with a mitt for extra polishing power or simply massage it over your body and face with your hands, then rinse. Do this once a week for a radiant complexion.

soaps

There are many different types of soap manufactured today, all of which offer unique properties and are available in myriad shapes and finishes – soft, creamy bars and grainy handmade slabs with a rough-hewn texture and finish, vividly coloured cubes and smooth, tactile pebbles. Whether you stack glossy transparent blocks on a windowsill to catch the light or pile pretty pastel bars into a ceramic bowl or wicker basket, a collection of soaps that smell delicious can make a simple but striking feature.

Today, the most popular soaps are inspired by nature. They are made of vegetable oils, rather than animal fats, and are packed with natural botanical ingredients. Plant-based soaps are very soft, creamy and conditioning to the skin. Olive oil, almond oil, avocado oil and grapeseed oil will help to keep the skin smooth and supple, and also have anti-ageing qualities. When these soaps are imbued with pure essential oils they offer added benefits – lavender, for instance, is very healing to the skin, tea tree is antibacterial and lemon is uplifting. These skin-friendly soaps, deliciously scented with extracts of herbs, flowers, spices and wood, include Marseilles soap, Bonne Mère soap and honey soap.

Soaps fragranced with warm, woody scents, such as juniper wood, pear wood and lemon wood, are reminiscent of the fresh, earthy aromas of a rain-washed forest.

Every household in France owns at least one bar of Marseilles soap. It evokes the immaculate whiteness of bed linen drying on the grass in the sun, of singing and laughter punctuated by the beating of sheets.

Marseilles soap is a traditional household soap that is often found in kitchens. It contains high quantities of olive oil or grapeseed oil, making it either green or white in colour respectively, and is often enhanced by the addition of natural minerals and fragrances such as chestnut and lavender. Marseilles soap was traditionally used for washing clothes; it is very efficient at cleansing the skin and can even gently remove tar.

Bonne Mère soaps are deliciously scented beauty soaps that are suitable for all skin types. Look out for formulas containing extracts of fresh Indian verbena, which has a tangy, zesty scent, or sweet almond milk, which is especially gentle and suitable for children.

Soaps containing honey are very gentle and moisturizing for the skin and can be used on both the face and body. Linden honey soap, which may also contain royal jelly, is a good choice for dry, sensitive skins and pine honey soap for combination and oily skins; acacia honey soap is suitable for all skin types.

Standard toiletry soaps tend to be rather hard and should not be used on the face due to their high pH number – they have a pH of 10 while the maximum pH of the skin is no higher than 6. Using this type of soap on the face strips the skin of its natural oils, which can have a number of ill effects. On oily skin, repeated use can lead to the production of excess oil (sebum); sensitive skin may become red and inflamed; dry skin will simply become more dehydrated.

Soap lasts longer when it is allowed to dry after use, so never leave water in the soap dish.

Very dry skin may be happier when it is cleansed with a moisturizing soap-free bar or foaming gel. These cleansers are very soft, creamy and conditioning, and cause a much smaller change in the pH balance of the skin, enabling it to recover more quickly and so leaving it less exposed to the elements.

If you have oily skin, look out for non-comedogenic beauty bars which won't block the pores. Creamy soaps are not suitable for you as they will be high in fats and oils.

Strong antibacterial soaps should be used on the hands only – and occasionally – because they tend to be very dehydrating to the skin.

Finely ground particles of mother-of-pearl are often added to make soap particularly silky.

Extra-moisturizing and mild soap containing shea butter can be used as a beauty soap on the face. Look for formulas containing honey and milk.

Grainy, exfoliating soaps, many of which contain oatmeal to lightly scrub the skin, are effective for buffing the dead cells off a more mature, dry skin. This enables moisturizers to penetrate the surface more easily. However, these soaps may be too stimulating for sensitive or breakout-prone skin.

The moulds for Marseilles soap – which comes in large super-slippery cubes – are becoming highly collectable. The classic bee, text, and other designs can be found in junk shops and antique shops throughout Provence.

pur végétal
125
GRAMMES
Made in France
SAVON
de la
BONNE
MÈRE
MARSEILLE

Spring and Summer Morning Bath

This blend will gently wake you up and refresh you. Add to a tablespoon of carrier oil:

3 drops lemon essential oil
3 drops grapefruit essential oil
2 drops lime essential oil

Winter Reviver

These oils have antidepressant qualities that will help beat the winter blues. Add to a tablespoon of carrier oil:

4 drops rosemary essential oil
3 drops bergamot essential oil
3 drops rosewood essential oil

Cold Fighter

To help clear the respiratory tract and combat infection. Add to a tablespoon of carrier oil:

4 drops marjoram essential oil
3 drops eucalyptus essential oil
2 drops jasmine essential oil

aromatherapy bathing

To maximize the physical and spiritual benefits of your bath, add a few drops of essential oils. These highly concentrated essences, which are extracted from flowers, trees and herbs, have been used for thousands of years for their therapeutic effects on the mind and body. The tiny molecules of oil, which are absorbed into the bloodstream directly through the skin and by the capillaries in the lungs when the aromatic vapours are inhaled, have been shown scientifically to have specific actions on the balance of the psyche, the condition of the skin and the efficiency of the internal organs of the body. Bathing is a particularly effective way of using essential oils because they can enter the body by both absorption and inhalation.

Essential oils are far too potent to be used undiluted; they should always be added to a bubble bath, a vegetable carrier oil, such as sweet almond oil or grapeseed oil, or a neutral cream or lotion before coming into contact with the skin. Many oils, such as lavender, camomile and marjoram, are highly relaxing and stress-relieving and can help to encourage sleepiness. Others, such as grapefruit, rosemary and peppermint, are refreshing and stimulating and will help to encourage good circulation – thereby aiding detoxification – as well as increase your concentration and clarity of thought; these essences are best used in the morning. All essential oils have been found to have a profoundly positive, balancing and uplifting effect on the mood and emotions.

Dilute no more than the recommended number of drops of essential oil – up to a maximum of 10 drops in total if you are blending different oils – in a tablespoon of carrier oil or bath foam and pour it under warm running water. Close the door to keep the fragrant steam in the room, and swirl the water to distribute the oils thoroughly before you step in. Lie back, close your eyes and soak for about 20 minutes, breathing deeply to inhale the vapours and help the oils travel to the mood centre of the brain.

As long as you don't have very sensitive skin, you can use essential oils in the shower by diluting 4 drops in a tablespoon of carrier oil and pouring it onto a flannel. Rub the sides of the flannel together to distribute the mixture evenly, then sweep it vigorously over your skin while standing under the jet of water.

You can use the oils singly or in blends, but never exceed the stated number of drops – the blends given here are suitable for adults only. Several essential oils should be avoided during pregnancy, if you have high blood pressure or epilepsy, or if you suffer from a skin condition such as eczema or psoriasis. Read the Aromatherapy chapter on page 122 for further information on individual oils and their properties.

fragrant foam baths

Aromatic foam baths and shower gels that contain ready-blended essential oils will have an uplifting effect on the mind, but their therapeutic benefits will not be as powerful as those of pure essential oils. However – floral or herbal, citrus or sweet – they smell gorgeous and there is nothing more luxurious than sinking into a warm, scented bath, brimming with pure white foam.

To help revitalize you in the morning, use a fresh, invigorating scent like green tea or verbena, and to help calm you come the evening, try lavender or rosewood. For the perfect summertime bath, soak in fruity peach or magnolia, and in winter a bubble bath containing warming cinnamon or peppermint will help keep colds and chills at bay. For an exotic bath, scent the water with extracts of honeysuckle, lotus flower or jasmine, and for the ultimate in escapism, sprinkle a handful of fragrant petals into the water and let your imagination carry you away.

Bath water should be body temperature. Water that is too hot will overstimulate the body and cause the heart to pound – it could also break the tiny blood capillaries in the legs leading, eventually, to thread veins.

Avoid soaking in the bath for longer than about 20 minutes, or the skin will become overhydrated and look as wrinkly as a prune.

detoxifying bath salts

Sea salt is packed with beneficial minerals that can be absorbed and metabolized by the body, and using scented bath salts is a great way to aid detoxification and leave the skin deliciously soft and fragrant. The salts work by osmosis, drawing the toxins out of the body through the skin and helping to balance the levels of potassium and magnesium. As a generous helping of fragrant salts are sprinkled under warm running water, the volatile essential oils with which they are impregnated are released by the heat and give a boost to flagging spirits.

Get back to nature and wallow in a herbal bath infused with your own 'bouquet garni' made from a mixture of scented dried flowers and herbs gathered up in a mini muslin bag. Try camomile, lavender, rosemary and marjoram.

herbal baths

In American Indian culture, bathing is part of the process of spiritual rebirth. 'Vapour baths' are constructed inside the huts to create a sauna-style environment that opens the pores and helps to cleanse them of impurities. Fires are built in the centre of the floor, and stones are heated and then covered with water that has been infused with plants such as lavender and sage. These herbs have been used for centuries for their ability to dispel negative energy and evil spirits in a process known as 'space clearing'. To create a similar effect in a modern sauna, add a couple of drops of a cleansing and detoxifying essential oil, such as pine, eucalyptus or tea tree, to the water that is poured over the hot coals. These oils also have antiseptic and antibacterial properties, which are beneficial in a communal sauna. The heat from the coals will vaporize the highly volatile essential oils and disperse them into the hot steam. Breathe deeply to inhale the aromatic vapour.

If you like the idea of a natural herbal bath, use a mixture of fragrant dried herbs to make a bath 'tea bag'. Wrap a blend of your chosen flowers or leaves in a piece of loose-weave fabric such as muslin or cheesecloth and tie it securely with a pretty ribbon. Hang the herbal sachet under the tap so that running water will flow over it and submerge it once the bathtub is full. The warm water will encourage the plant extracts to diffuse through the fabric. Lavender, camomile flowers, marjoram, rose petals and pine needles all make wonderful fragrant infusions. Add a drop or two of the corresponding essential oils to the dried mixture to enhance the scent and therapeutic benefits. If you have dry skin, include oat flakes or oatbran, which have a moisturizing and softening effect on the skin, together with the herb mixture and squeeze the sachet gently under the water to encourage the goodness to disperse.

post-ablution treats

The pampering shouldn't stop once you get out of the bath. Gently pat your skin dry with a soft, warm towel spritzed with fragrant water to give it a delicate scent. Before you wrap yourself in your robe, continue the sensuous experience by slathering yourself with a hydrating lotion to seal in the moisture, massaging your limbs with toning oil or spritzing your body with an invigorating splash.

Crystal deodorants are something of a natural miracle and will keep you super-dry. They contain none of the pore-blocking aluminium found in other types of deodorants and antiperspirants, and complementary therapists recommend them because they do not impede the lymph system around the breast area. Simply run the block of solid crystal under the tap and apply it under the arms.

For the ultimate refresher, take a leaf out of the beauty books of women who live in hot climates and apply an invigorating body splash. A good body splash will be alcohol-free, so that it is not drying to the skin, and will contain a combination of essential oils to leave skin silky-smooth and delicately scented. You simply rub it over the body after a bath or shower.

COLD CREAM
15%
L'OCCITANE
17 S

Cellulite Buster

30 ml sweet almond oil
4 drops cypress essential oil
3 drops grapefruit essential oil
3 drops juniper essential oil
2 drops lemon essential oil

Energizing Oil Blend

30 ml grapeseed or apricot kernel oil
4 drops bergamot essential oil
3 drops lavender essential oil
2 drops juniper essential oil
1 drop peppermint essential oil

Moisturizer for Dry or Sensitive Skin

30 ml sweet almond or macadamia nut oil
4 drops patchouli essential oil
3 drops rose essential oil
2 drops frankincense essential oil
2 drops sandalwood essential oil

massage oils

Either use a ready-mixed massage oil base or blend your own using one or more vegetable oils, such as grapeseed oil, sweet almond oil, apricot kernel oil, macadamia nut oil or jojoba oil (see page 46). These base oils have skin-softening, nourishing and anti-ageing properties – even before you add essential oils. Grapeseed oil, for instance, protects against the harmful effects of free radicals and sweet almond oil can help to alleviate irritated, dry skin. A good standard base oil that is suitable for most skin types can be made from 30 ml of sweet almond oil and 5 drops each of jojoba and carrot oils. To this, add your chosen blend of essential oils (see recipes opposite).

A home-made massage oil blend should be made up to a concentration of no more than two per cent. 1 ml of carrier oil is approximately 20 drops, so add a maximum of 1 drop of essential oil for every 2.5 ml of vegetable oil.

Try an altogether different secret that will leave your skin fabulously smooth and sensual. Dry body oil is a totally non-greasy formula with a very light, fluid texture that makes it easily absorbed. It is sprayed on to the skin to leave a softening, lightly scented sheen.

creams

Drinking plenty of filtered or bottled water will undoubtedly help keep your skin hydrated, but environmental factors such as sun, wind, air conditioning and central heating inevitably have a drying effect. Applying a good all-over moisturizing cream after bathing takes only a few moments and can make all the difference. Aside from the therapeutic and mood-enhancing benefits, achieving soft, sensual, sweet-smelling skin is one of the great pleasures of incorporating essential oil products into your bathtime routine. Nourishing body creams that contain key moisturizing and conditioning ingredients such as shea butter and milk extracts, with added essences, such as ylang ylang and lavender to reduce tension, and neroli to strengthen mature or fragile skins, are wonderful skin-smoothers. However, you can also blend your own hydrating concoction by adding your chosen blend of essences to a neutral, natural cream base.

Shea butter is a dream come true if you have dry, dehydrated skin or damaged hair. It is extracted from the nut of the shea tree that is native to Central Africa. There, the harvesting of the fruit and nuts is the domain of women and the money they make is exclusively for them 'shea' is literally 'women's gold'. The highest quality nuts are needed in order to make the finest products. The women of Burkina Fass are able to distinguish between the 'vintage' shea, which is used for cosmetics, and the shea that can be used for cooking and eating.

When you touch a shea butter product, you understand immediately why it is so sought-after. It is the silkiest of emollients, and it doesn't feel heavy when it is applied to the skin or hair. Warm a small amount of concentrated shea butter in your hand and rub it over extra-dry places, such as elbows, knees and heels. In addition to its super-hydrating effects, shea butter has proven healing and regenerating properties; it boosts the skin's elasticity and helps ease painful joints.

shea butter products

Shea butter soaps fragranced with, for example, wild rose, verbena and clementine, may also contain either sweet almond oil (suitable for all skin types), milk (suitable for children), honey and calendula (extra-moisturizing), or rosemary (which has antiseptic qualities making it suitable for combination and oily skins).

Rich shea butter shower cream can contain skin-regenerating soya protein and may be used on the body and hair.

Detergent-free liquid soaps are made very mild and moisturizing by the inclusion of shea butter.

One or two bath pearls containing 45 per cent shea butter can be added to running water to deliver a heavenly bathtime experience.

Shea butter massage balm comprises 60 per cent shea butter, and may also include essences of pine, eucalyptus, camphor and peppermint. It is ideal for use after sport, or simply as an aid to relaxation.

hands and nails

Like your face, your hands are always on display and exposed to the elements, so they will be one of the first parts of your body to show signs of ageing. There's something very gratifying about looking after your hands and nails. This has a lot to do with the fact that they are quick to respond to care and attention – and they offer a way of lavishing a little luxury on yourself relatively cheaply.

Book yourself in for a professional manicure and ask for advice on improving the condition of your nails. Normal nails are strong, pink and flexible with smooth nail plates. Dry nails lack lustre and may have ridges; they are crying out for moisture. Dehydrated nails may flake – nails become dehydrated with age. Brittle nails are hard, inflexible, and easily crack or chip; most of all they need oil. Damaged nails are caused by overuse of artificial nails or a sensitivity to the products which have been used on them; they are often soft, lacking in lustre, and may also peel or flake.

ten-minute manicure

Start by massaging a softening hand scrub all over the hands and wrists. A shea butter-enriched formula is suitable even for sensitive skins.

Remove all traces of polish or handcream from the nails using a remover that is acetone-free. Real cotton wool (instead of synthetic) will absorb enamel more easily and doesn't contain stray fibres that can adhere to polish.

Use an emery board to shape the nails. File gently in one direction only, from the outside in. Don't see-saw the file backwards and forwards.

Apply a cuticle remover and soak one hand at a time in warm soapy water.

Gently push the cuticles back with the rubber end of a hoof stick. Rinse the nails with clean warm water and dry them thoroughly.

Apply a protective base coat and allow it to dry.

Sweep on your first coat of nail polish in four strokes. Let it dry before applying a second coat in the same way.

When the second coat is dry, complete with a top coat for a high-gloss finish.

dos and don'ts

Don't file down the sides of the nails as you will weaken them. Use a soft-cushioned nail file, not one of metal.

Don't put your hands in water containing household chemicals and always apply handcream after washing your hands.

Do use cuticle remover once a week. Use a rubber hoof stick to gently push the cuticles back; don't cut them.

Do keep cuticle oil or cream by your bed and apply it every night.

Don't apply nail hardeners without advice from a manicurist, and only use them as a short-term treatment or the nails may become too hard and inflexible. If your nails are soft and peeling, use a hardener containing protein and calcium, or have a paraffin wax or hot-oil mitt treatment.

Don't buff your nails too often.

Do exfoliate your hands with a hand, face or body scrub, then use an oil or rich cream treatment.

Don't skip vitamin-enriched base and top coats if you want your manicure to last. These provide a protective seal for weak and damaged nails.

Do apply polish in four strokes, the first across the base of the nail, the next in the centre and the last two along the sides. Leave a fine line along the sides of the nail on the first coat but cover the entire nail on the second coat. A good polish should have a firm brush that delivers just the right amount of colour.

Don't bath or shower for six hours after a manicure.

Don't simply team your nail polish with your outfit; take your skin tone into account, too.

Do keep a stock of nail plasters; these will hold a torn nail in place for up to a week.

Don't forget your feet. Once a week use a pumice stone or foot file on hard skin and exfoliate the feet with a scrub; apply a rich moisturizer after bathing. Avoid in-growing toenails by cutting the nails straight across.

skincare

When it comes to looking after your skin, a little regular care goes a long way to maintaining a fresh, healthy-looking complexion. Discover how to make up moisturizing and revitalizing aromatherapy oils and masks that are tailored to your skin type, and learn about the plant extracts and botanicals that will give your skin what it needs. It will thank you for it.

'It was on the way back from Nîmes, on a July afternoon. The heat was unendurable. The blazing white of the road, an esplanade of dust amid the olive groves and young oaks, stretched out into the distance beneath the dull silver of a sun which filled the sky. Not a trace of shade, not a breath of wind.'

Alphonse Daudet, *Letters from my Mill*

Whether your skin is exposed to the relentless heat, sun and dust of a hot climate or you have to cope with the inevitable grime of a city, the condition of your skin mirrors your lifestyle. If you have a hectic stress-filled schedule, are exposed to pollution, sunbathe or smoke, your skin is more vulnerable to premature ageing and to developing problems like acne. When skin goes awry, life can seem impossibly difficult. Outbreaks of spots and rashes send even the most level-headed person into paroxysms of despair. The subject can engender untold angst, passion and pleasure – to hear a woman discuss a new-found skincare regime that excites her is to witness her femininity, her recognition that her skin is one of her most precious assets.

Research has shown that many women spend very little time each day caring for themselves, regarding 'me-time' as a luxury and feeling guilty if they are not working or caring for their family and friends. But it's important to believe that following a skincare regime is a necessity, not a luxury.

the beauty regime

When you pay attention to your inner health – your physical, emotional and spiritual wellbeing – you will find that your outer beauty reaps the benefit. Your diet should include at least five portions of fruit and vegetables a day (preferably organic) because they contain antioxidants that will help to protect the skin from ageing. Drink six to eight glasses of filtered or bottled water every day, and consider consulting a trained nutritional therapist in order to work out a vitamin and mineral supplementation programme.

Naturopathic therapists and physicians also emphasize the importance of daily exercise and of getting outside into the light and air. Exercise increases the flow of oxygen and blood to the cells, which feeds the skin and hair with nutrients. It also reduces levels of stress hormones in the body and increases the production of mood-boosting chemicals.

Your skincare routine should:

Cleanse the skin – a good cleansing system has the power to actually improve the condition of the skin.

Protect the skin from the elements.

Deliver moisture to the surface of the skin and help prevent it from escaping.

Revitalize, condition and nourish the skin by providing it with all the nutrients it needs to keep it healthy, and stimulate cell renewal with active anti-ageing ingredients to help it remain fresh-looking for longer.

You should also apply a face mask and exfoliate at least once a week to nourish the skin and encourage its renewal. Sloughing off the dead cells that sit on the surface stimulates cell regeneration and allows the skin to reflect light more effectively, so you emerge with a glowing, smoother complexion.

A good way to understand your skin and discover the products that will keep it at its best is to have a professional consultation and facial. Increasingly, beauticians are trained in holistic therapies like aromatherapy, reflexology and lymph drainage, and they will be able to bring this experience to your programme.

It is important to recognize that your skin's needs change from week to week and from season to season. So although your basic skin type – normal, dry, oily or combination – remains the same throughout your life, its requirements are affected by many internal and external factors – ageing, hormonal changes, exposure to pollution and to the sun, living in central-heated and air-conditioned rooms, for example. The home spa skincare plans (pages 48–55) are tailored to meet these various and changing requirements.

Modern life is tough on skin. When your emotions, stress levels and hormones are on a roller coaster, your skin will follow. Luckily, it is possible to balance the ups and downs, the highs and lows.

key ingredients

Essential oils extracted from plants are some of the most active ingredients known to cosmetologists. In many cases, only minute quantities are required of these very potent essences and they should always be blended with a carrier cream or oil first. Essences extracted from citrus fruits or blossoms should not be used before exposure to the sun. You should also consult a trained aromatherapist if you are pregnant or taking medication.

One hour before applying a home-blended massage oil, mask, moisturizer or toner, check that you will not develop a sensitivity to it. Apply a little to the side of your face and make sure no rash or soreness develops. If you have very sensitive skin, it is advisable to do this patch test 24 hours beforehand.

Bergamot Soothing for skin conditions like acne and eczema; don't use it before exposure to the sun, as it may cause burning.
Camomile German and Roman Camomile are very useful in treating dry skin, eczema and rashes.
Frankincense A balancing oil that can help treat acne; it also has rejuvenating properties and is beneficial to ageing skin.
Geranium This oil balances sebum production and can be used for dry or oily skins.
Lavender A very healing oil that is used to treat burns, sunburn, insect bites, spots and acne.
Neroli Good for normal to sensitive skins.
Rosewood Softening for dry skin.
Sandalwood An anti-inflammatory and healing oil used to help treat acne, very dry skin and eczema.
Tea Tree An antiseptic oil good for acne, spots and dandruff.

There is a wide range of carrier oils to which essences can be added for application – some are more suitable for dry skins, others for oily skins. Nut oils tend to be thicker and need to be warmed up in the hands before application.

Apricot Kernel A light oil that penetrates easily and is suitable for all skin types. It contains high levels of vitamin A, which can increase the production of collagen (part of the skin's support network).
Grapeseed A light oil that is high in protein and the antioxidants that help fight the ageing process. It is especially good for oily and combination skins.
Jojoba Regenerating for all skin types and calming for irritated or inflamed skin.
Macadamia Nut Rich in vitamins A, E and F, this oil is good for dry skin and regenerating for ageing skin.
Peach Kernel This contains high levels of vitamin A and is used to treat dry, sun-damaged skin and stretch marks.
Safflower Good for all skin types, it contains vitamins, minerals and proteins.
Soya Bean A light oil that nourishes oily skins and contains vitamins and proteins.
Sweet Almond Best for dry skin and helpful for relieving itching or inflammation.
Wheatgerm Rich in proteins and vitamin E, it is balancing for all skin types and is revitalizing for prematurely aged skin.

Floral waters – infusions of petals and flowers – are lightly scented and make refreshing, gentle toners. They can be used alone or with the addition of a few drops of essential oil to enhance their therapeutic action. Their delightful aromas lift the spirits while the flower extracts help balance the skin.

Rosewater The slightly astringent properties make it ideal for combination and oily skins.
Cornflower Water A decongestant and soothing water that can be applied to puffy eyes on a cotton-wool compress.
Orange Blossom Water A soothing water for normal, dry and sensitive skins; it can also be used on children.

normal skin

Your skin is naturally:

Firm and supple
Smooth-textured with no signs of open pores
Velvety to the touch
Fresh and transparent-looking if you are a blonde

Remove any make-up and dirt with a wipe-off cleanser – massage the cleanser gently into the complexion with your fingers and wipe the excess away with a cotton-wool pad.

Remove any traces of cleanser with an alcohol-free toner such as orange blossom water.

Use a moisturizing face mask to promote radiance. A suitable mask may combine essential oils of lemon, eucalyptus, juniper and lavender with peach extract, ginseng and highly moisturizing shea butter. Apply the mask to the skin, avoiding the eye area, and leave it for 10 minutes before wiping it off with cotton wool.

Apply a moisturizing day or night lotion that also includes stimulating ingredients such as ylang ylang and musk-rose oil.

Moisturizer for Normal Skin

To maintain the balance of a normal skin:

20 ml of wheatgerm or peach kernel oil
3 drops neroli essential oil
3 drops lavender essential oil
2 drops geranium essential oil
2 drops frankincense essential oil

combination or oily skin

You may find that:

Your skin feels comparatively thick and strong
Skin is shiny around the T-zone (forehead, nose and chin)
Some pores may look open
Your make-up will not last well

The build-up of excess sebum – the skin's natural oil – will lead to open pores and acne, so it is important to cleanse oily skin thoroughly but gently so as not to cause irritation and to help it stay in balance. Use a foaming gel with purifying essential oils such as peppermint, cypress and lemon.

Witch hazel and rosemary extract will tone the skin, while zinc will help to balance the acid mantle. An alcohol-free clarifying toner will refresh the complexion.

Mask for Combination or Oily Skin

This mask has a purifying and exfoliating action:

20 ml soya oil
4 drops geranium essential oil
3 drops camomile essential oil
2 drops sandalwood essential oil
1 drop lavender essential oil

Leave the mask on for 10 minutes, then remove it gently with a cotton-wool pad and tone with rosewater.

If you suffer from spots or acne, use a lotion that can be applied directly to help dry out spots. A lotion that contains camphor oil is especially suitable as it has antiseptic qualities, while lavender oil will calm and heal the area. Look for oil-free moisturizers which will be light in texture.

tired, dull skin

You may find that:

- Your skin is lacking in elasticity and firmness
- Expression lines and wrinkles are more marked
- Your complexion lacks radiance and looks dull

With age, skin has a greater tendency to look dull, grey and tired. Cell turnover diminishes gradually after the age of 25, so it is important to use natural ingredients that will promote this.

Use a cleanser, toner and mask designed for dry, sensitive skin to maintain the moisture levels in the upper layers of the skin.

Before you apply moisturizer, smooth on a firming serum that will reduce the appearance of small wrinkles and expression lines. Soya protein and *Mimosa terriflora* (which is known as the 'skin tree' and is renowned for its healing and revitalizing capabilities) will firm up and repair the skin and provide good protection from ageing free radicals.

Use an intensive, restructuring moisturizer to continue the firming and repairing action.

Mask or Massage Blend for Tired Skin

Apply as a mask for 10 minutes or massage onto the face:

- 24 ml apricot kernel oil
- 5 drops petitgrain essential oil
- 4 drops sandalwood essential oil
- 3 drops camomile essential oil

papery skin

Your skin is:

- Sensitive, fragile and papery to the touch
- Fine-textured with no visible pores
- Prone to developing fine lines and wrinkles

Skin may become dry and vulnerable to ageing particles in the atmosphere when the weather turns cold, since a lack of moisture can lead to cracking (invisible to the naked eye), impairing its natural protection.

Use a mild cleanser with ingredients such as marsh mallow to help repair damage. Shea butter and geranium, rosewood and bitter orange essential oils will leave the skin supple.

A calming spray of camomile and orange blossom waters, and honey and nectar extracts will soothe, tone and help prolong hydration.

Exfoliate dry, papery skin with a rich mask. Oatmeal and white clay provide a gentle, refining action.

A hypo-allergenic cream containing evening primrose oil to stimulate cell renewal and moisturizing agents derived from sugar and nectar will strengthen the protective barrier.

Massage Oil for Dry, Papery Skin

Use this replenishing blend for a facial massage (see page 56):

- 24 ml jojoba oil
- 4 drops neroli essential oil
- 3 drops patchouli essential oil
- 3 drops sandalwood essential oil
- 2 drops rose or rosewood essential oil

sun-damaged skin

Your skin may show:

- Surface dryness
- An increase in pigmentation marks over time
- Loss of firmness and increased wrinkles

Or, if you have naturally oily or combination skin:

- An excess production of sebum and spots

The jury is out on whether the skin's number-one enemy is the sun or pollution and cigarette smoke. What is certain is that they wreak havoc with the skin and are major causes of premature ageing. In fact, the skin can appear to age almost overnight when the body's repair systems start to slow down.

The good news is that when it is adequately protected from the sun, the skin is able to repair itself by up to 35 per cent. This means that you need to wear a moisturizer that contains a UVA and UVB sunscreen throughout the summer months, or all year round if you live in a sunny climate. Plant extracts and vitamins are increasingly included in suncare formulations because they can help the skin to fend off the onslaught of free radicals (the highly unstable molecules which damage cells and lead to loss of firmness and, ultimately, wrinkling).

If you are spending longer than 15 minutes in direct sunlight, high-factor sunscreens are essential for all except the darkest skins. Using a high factor sun-screen does not mean that you should bake in the sun for hours, and remember that you are exposed to the sun's rays even when you are in the shade or wearing clothing that is not SPF-rated. Bear in mind, too, that the dangerous effects of the sun's rays are intensified when you are swimming, since the rays are reflected off the water and can penetrate wet skin more easily. Ageing UVA rays can even penetrate through glass, so protect yourself when driving.

after-sun care

If you have accidentally overexposed yourself to the sun, soothe the skin with the following strategies:

- Red, burning skin is best treated with camomile oil, according to aromatherapist Patricia Davis. Take a lukewarm bath with 5 or 6 drops of camomile essence diluted in a tablespoon of carrier oil. Repeat this at intervals of a few hours until the burning subsides.

- Severe sunburn should be treated with lavender oil. Make a solution of lavender oil in boiled and cooled water, adding 12 drops of essence for each tablespoon of water. Dab this onto the skin where it is not blistered or broken. Lavender essence can be applied neat if there are blisters. Severe sunburn may require medical attention.

If your skin is dry and flaking after exposure to the elements, gently exfoliate it using a scrub or a mask to remove the surface dryness, then apply a healing, moisturizing treatment.

- Apply a drop of undiluted tea tree oil to spots if the sun has triggered the production of excess sebum.

Protect your skin from the elements all year round, using ingredients to hydrate, replenish and repair.

eye care

The eye zone is the most sensitive and fragile area of the face, and the super-thin skin is subject to a great deal of stress. The eyes are the first place to show tiredness and fatigue is always more evident in this area of the face. Sometimes the most obvious things – like getting more rest and consciously putting your batteries on charge following a period of extra stress – are the simplest and most effective ways to make yourself look and feel 100 per cent better. However, to keep signs of ageing a bay, it is essential to take the time to care for your eyes on a daily basis.

Do remove eye make-up as gently as possible. A remover that contains cornflower water will soothe and moisturize the delicate skin. Soak a cotton-wool pad and hold it onto the eye and lashes, with your eyes closed, for about 30 seconds (using a separate pad for each eye). This will help dissolve the mascara and so prevent you from rubbing the skin. Gently remove the make-up by sweeping the pad outwards on the top lids and then in towards the corner of the eye to clean the lower lids. Remember that long-lasting make-up requires a special-formula remover for the job.

Do apply an eye contour gel every morning. It should contain anti-ageing vitamins, such as vitamin E and sun filters; it may also include toning and moisturizing plant extracts, such as lemon, lavender or mandarin. Dab the gel on using the ring (fourth) finger and then rhythmically tap around the eye zone until it is absorbed.

Do use a skin-repairing eye cream in the evening, applying just a minimal amount.

Don't apply your regular moisturizer to the eye area as it will be too rich and may trigger a reaction.

When your eyes feel tired, try the 'palming' method to refresh them. Simply cup your hands and place your palms over your closed eyes. Breathe in and out slowly for a minute or two.

When you are working on a computer or doing detailed work, look away into the distance every 15 minutes.

Cooling Eye Reviver

To refresh and brighten tired eyes, steep two round cotton-wool pads in some extra-gentle cornflower water that has been kept in the fridge. Lie down and apply the damp pads to your closed eyes for 5 minutes. This will help to reduce under-eye circles and puffiness and is perfect for use before a party. If you want to minimize fine lines or crow's feet, use a little macadamia nut oil instead of cornflower water, but apply it to the under-eye area only.

Never attempt to blend your own products containing essential oils for use around the eyes.

Try soaking two cotton-wool pads in cool witch hazel and apply them to the eyes to refresh and awaken.

the home spa facial

On the most basic level, massaging the skin on your face will help to release tension in the muscles and can be a supremely soothing and relaxing experience. It also increases micro-circulation, which aids the delivery of nutrients to the cells and improves lymphatic drainage. This is especially beneficial to the appearance of the skin, since it is the lymph system that drains excess fluid from the cells, reducing any tendency to puffiness.

Begin by cleansing your face thoroughly using either a cleansing lotion or a facial wash suitable for your skin type, and gently remove any eye make-up.

To help stimulate the lymph system, use your fingertips to massage around the perimeter of your ears for one minute using small circular motions.

Work your way down the side of your face and neck to your breastbone, finishing just above your breasts.

Apply a replenishing serum to the skin, or an aromatherapy oil blend that is made up of essential oils and a light moisturizing base oil. Start in the centre of your forehead between your eyes and, using the first and second fingers of each hand, rhythmically stroke your forehead using light, upward movements. Alternating hands, move out to one side of your forehead and work your way slowly across to the other side and then back to the centre.

Place your first and second fingers along the sides of your nose and gently press, working outwards across your cheekbones towards your hairline. Repeat six times, moving down your face as you do so.

When you reach your chin, use your thumbs and first fingers to pinch the skin along the jawbone, working from the centre of the chin to the sides of the face.

Gently pinch along the length of each eyebrow, starting in the centre and working outwards. Repeat several times.

Finish by closing your eyes and placing the pads of your first two fingers to your temples; hold for five seconds and repeat.

Apply a face mask suitable for your skin's needs and leave it on for 10 minutes or as directed.

After thoroughly removing the mask, apply a refreshing eye gel to the eye area and a moisturizer to your face and neck, smoothing it upwards from your chest.

Give your face the ultimate treat, improve circulation and purify, refresh and rejuvenate the skin.

haircare

Symbolically, our hair is incredibly important to us. It speaks volumes to others of our personal style and taste, and it can be a sign of wellbeing and good health. It also offers great potential for change – every hairdresser will tell you that when a woman's relationship breaks up, a dramatic hair cut is likely to follow.

'Modern, effective hair care must be holistic – it must take into account your entire lifestyle – your past and present, your future plans and hopes, how you presently live and how you seek to change your life.'

Philip Kingsley, *The Complete Hair Book*

The condition of your hair is greatly affected by the food you eat and the lifestyle you live. Irregular eating habits or a diet lacking in key nutrients can lead to hair thinning and even hair loss. Many women find that when they correct poor eating habits, such as skipping meals, the condition of their hair – which is the last in the body's queue for nutrients – greatly improves. If you have naturally greasy hair, check that your diet is not high in saturated animal fats. If you have dry hair, ensure that you are eating adequate fish oils and vegetable oils, such as olive oil and safflower oil, which are rich in essential fatty acids.

Stress, too, can have a dramatic impact on the hair. It causes the tiny capillaries that feed the follicles to constrict and so reduces the quantities of oxygen and nutrients that reach the hair. Stress also affects the muscles at the point where the hair grows out of the scalp and can, over time, lead to excessive hair loss. Levels of the androgen hormone, which is associated with the thinning of hair generally found in men, may increase, and an excessive production of sweat, which may also be caused by stress, will make the hair and scalp greasy.

brushing & combing

It is advisable to brush your hair morning and evening to remove any airborne pollutants and dry flakes from the scalp, and to distribute oil down the hair shaft. Dry hair will benefit from brushing more than greasy hair for this reason. However, you should not overbrush: 100 strokes a day may lead to split ends.

Always use a comb on wet hair, never a brush, as the hair is much more elastic when wet and more vulnerable to breaking. Use a wide-toothed comb to distribute conditioner evenly through the hair, which will help the individual hair shafts to absorb the proteins it contains. Untangle any knots starting at the ends of the hair and gradually working upwards.

long hair

You need a rubber-backed brush with metal 'bristles' that will enable you to untangle knots without tugging or breaking the hair. A paddle- or oval-shaped brush provides a greater surface area, allowing the brush to travel through the hair more easily.

If you are blow-drying your hair you will find it easier to use a fat, round brush, as you can hook the ends of the hair under the brush and hold it straight as you dry it. There should be rounded ends to the bristles to protect the hair from splitting. The rubber backing will help the brush to be anti-static.

medium-length hair

Look for a rubber-backed brush with specially tapered, natural bristles. The longer bristles untangle the hair, while the shorter ones smooth the cuticle.

short hair

The best choice is a rectangular brush with natural bristles in two lengths. Rubber backing is not essential as static is not such a problem as it is with longer hair.

curly and wavy hair

Use a 'rake' specially designed for untangling thick, curly hair and a round, natural-bristle brush that is anti-static.

You can avoid any tendency to yellowness or brassiness on blonde or bleached hair by using a shampoo and conditioner that contain essential oil of lavender.

shampooing & conditioning

Regular shampooing and conditioning is vital for healthy hair. If you live in a city or have greasy hair, trichologists recommend daily shampooing to cleanse away pollution that will affect the condition of the scalp, and to prevent excess grease, which can create an oily, flaky scalp that may lead to thinning and hair loss.

It is important to use a good-quality shampoo, as this will contain gentle detergents that clean the hair but don't strip it of its natural oils. It should also contain proteins, vitamins, such as vitamins B5, E and F, and plant extracts, such as orange, rosemary and pine essential oils, which help improve the condition and strength of the hair, and combat free radicals. You need only a very small amount of a good shampoo and, if you wash your hair every day, one application will be sufficient.

Conditioner is essential for dry to normal hair and beneficial for greasy hair, although it should not be applied to the roots of greasy hair. Use a deep-conditioning hair treatment once a week if your hair is dry or chemically processed; applying it before a sauna or steam room session will help it to penetrate.

Hair Mask for all Hair Types

This recipe contains essential oils that help replace the hair's natural oils, making it shinier and silkier. Apply the mask before shampooing the hair and leave it on for 10 minutes. If the hair is very dry or has been chemically treated, use 20 ml of apricot kernel oil and add 10 ml of coconut oil to the mix.

30 ml apricot kernel oil
5 drops rose essential oil
4 drops camomile essential oil
3 drops ylang ylang essential oil
2 drops sandalwood essential oil

dry, damaged or colour-treated hair

Dry hair is the most vulnerable hair type because the hair shaft is less protected by sebum, making it susceptible to moisture loss and therefore liable to become brittle and dull-looking.

Hair that has been damaged by repeated use of overhot styling equipment, perming, or colour treatments and lighteners also tends to be extra-dry hair. Coloured and permed hair is especially porous and so takes longer to dry, which can lead to problems if you regularly use a hairdryer.

Shine-enhancing shampoo and conditioner that contain vegetable proteins are essential because they will help to rebuild the damaged areas of the hair shaft. Shea butter replenishes moisture, while essential oils such as lemon, verbena, orange and cypress will stimulate blood circulation to the scalp and so increase the flow of nutrients to the roots. Colour-treated hair is in need of specially formulated shampoo and conditioner to keep the colour fresh for longer.

Look for a hairdryer that has a heat-regulating mechanism, as some have been found to become super-hot during extended use, and don't overuse direct sources of heat, such as tongs, crimpers and straightening irons. Some styling products offer added protection against heat and can also reduce the porosity of the hair, reducing blow-drying time.

Gum, wax and pomade are best for styling thick dry hair, while shine-enhancing serum is a lighter option for fine dry hair. Mousse should be alcohol-free.

oily hair

Oily hair is naturally well protected from drying out and becoming fragile. However, if left unchecked, the greasy sebum can suffocate the scalp and even lead to increased hair loss.

Oily hair cries out for a purifying shampoo containing plant extracts, such as asebiol, recognized for its ability to restore balance to oil-prone hair. Other beneficial ingredients are the astringent essential oils of lemon, rosemary, peppermint and lavender.

Washing your hair every day is beneficial, as long as you use a good-quality shampoo and avoid applying conditioner near the roots.

Top trichologist Philip Kingsley recommends applying a solution of witch hazel and lemon to the roots of excessively oily hair after washing. Mix 225 ml of witch hazel, 225 ml of water (preferably distilled) and the juice of one lemon. While the hair is still damp, apply the solution along the parting using a cotton-wool ball. Make another parting and repeat the process until you have covered the entire scalp.

Hairspray is the best styling product for oily hair; avoid waxes and pomades which are too heavy and greasy.

A purifying hairspray containing lemon and lavender is a beauty life-saver, as it can banish the appearance of lank, oily hair as soon as it is applied. Spritz it on after towel-drying to keep your hair oil-free for longer.

curly hair

Curly hair is often dry and frizzy because the protective sebum is not distributed so easily along the hair shaft. In addition, the cuticle of the hair opens up where the hair kinks. Look out for styling products that will define the curl. One of the best ways to avoid frizziness is to apply serum to wet (not towel-dried) hair. Distribute it evenly using a wide-toothed comb and, if possible, let the hair dry naturally.

Thick curly hair has a tendency to become Big Hair, especially in damp weather. A super-hold styling lotion, bungee gum or wax will smooth the hair and define the curls while controlling them.

Fine curly hair is more prone to breakage than thick curly hair, so avoid overusing chemical treatments. Although colouring or perming helps to swell the hair shaft and so thicken the hair, it leaves the hair dry and more vulnerable.

A straightening lotion provides a protective barrier to the direct heat of straightening irons, which dramatically dries the hair. Steam straighteners take longer but are gentler.

Afro hair has the tightest curl because it grows out of a curved follicle. The outer cuticle is made up of between seven and eleven layers (Caucasian hair has four to seven layers), making it resistant to chemical processes. However, the inner cortex has less volume, so chemicals take effect more quickly. Shampoo and conditioner containing plant proteins, vitamins B5, E and F, and essential oils, such as sandalwood and ylang ylang, help to strengthen the cortex.

fine, limp or flyaway hair

Wispy, fine hair may be the bane of your life but there are ways to improve how you handle it. Use a volumizing shampoo that will also help to fortify the hair. Wheat proteins, quinine extract and essential oils, such as rosewood, lemon, geranium and verbena, will provide extra energy and vitality.

Use a detangling conditioner that will not weigh down the hair and apply it sparingly – most of us tend to use haircare products in much greater quantities than we really need.

Blunt cuts help to make fine hair look thicker.

Use body-building styling products, such as mousse or a liquid styling lotion that will increase the thickness of the hair shaft. Avoid gels, waxes and gums, as these are too heavy.

If your hair becomes dramatically thinner or you notice wider hair partings or increased hair loss, it is advisable to consult your doctor. There are a number of possible causes for hair loss, including eating irregularly or poor nutrition, stress, pregnancy, alopecia, or perhaps thyroid or hormonal problems.

New hair growth tends to stand up from the head, breaking the smooth silhouette of a sleek style. To tame these flyaway ends, use a styling lotion or serum tailored to your hair type, and the minimum of heat. Keep a small super-fine hairspray with you and consider wearing a hat in wet weather.

hair facts & tips

The hair shaft consists of three layers: the spongy central core, the medulla; the surrounding fibres, known as the cortex, which make up the bulk of the hair; and the overlapping outer layers of cells, the cuticle.

Hair grows at a rate of 1–1.5 cm (½–⅝ in) a month.

The life cycle of each hair is 3–7 years.

On average we have between 150,000 and 200,000 hairs.

We lose 40–100 hairs a day.

The layers of the hair shaft are made of the protein keratin. When the protein bonds are altered or broken, for instance, during perming or colouring, the hair becomes more susceptible to breakage.

Massaging the scalp will help to stimulate the production of oil and distribute it along the hair shaft. This is a trick which, if you have normal to dry hair, can be incorporated into your everyday shampoo session. If you have naturally oily hair, only massage your scalp occasionally – perhaps to relieve stress. Start at the forehead and, using all of the fingers and the thumbs of both hands, press and circle, feeling the scalp move beneath your fingers as you do so. Work from the front of the head towards the crown and then massage the back of the head. Finish by lightly stroking your hands rhythmically over your hair several times.

A treatment shampoo that contains Spanish juniper, tea tree, pine and eucalyptus will help to solve the problems of dandruff-prone hair. Alternate it with an extra-gentle shampoo.

Sun, wind, chlorine and salt water all spell disaster for dry or chemically treated hair. Sun can damage the hair's protein, while sea and pool water open up the cuticle, allowing moisture to escape. Use a conditioner that contains moisturizing, replenishing ingredients, such as shea butter, proteins and vitamins.

When you are on holiday, wear your hair in a ponytail or chignon to reduce the surface area that is exposed, or wear a hat or scarf.

If your hair is prone to frizziness, always use a conditioner and apply plenty of styling serum or hairspray before you go out in wet or humid weather.

Strand tests before perming or colouring are always advisable; hair that has been relaxed or bleached should not be permed.

Straightening or reducing the curl in Afro hair using a permanent process makes it easier to style, but the chemicals change the inner structure of the hair. The weight of longer hair helps to maintain a straightened look. Bristle brushes are recommended for relaxed hair, as a comb can adversely affect the hair's elasticity.

Avoid plaiting or weaving Afro hair too tightly; it can affect the hair follicles and cause scar tissue to form, which could lead to hair loss.

hair style

How you wear your hair – long or short, coloured or natural, curly and wild or sleek and straight – can reveal a great deal about your personality and way of life. Changing your hair style is probably the easiest, most dramatic and effective way of reinventing yourself.

First work out your overall look – the spirit of your individual style. Once that is understood, finding a haircut that can become your signature, a natural extension of your personality, becomes easier.

Of course, any style has to take account of your hair type and your lifestyle – a high-maintenance colour and cut don't usually go hand in hand with a frenetic schedule. After all, who has time to stand in front of the mirror with a hot brush or tongs when you've got a train to catch in the morning?

You may recognize yourself in some of the following personality traits:

the ingenue

You love to wear little fitted suits or chic cropped trousers, paired with pristine mannish shirts and elegant flat shoes. You have always admired Audrey Hepburn's sense of style. Your hair is cut boyishly short but styled flirtatiously with soft layers – a feminine version of the urchin cut.

the romantic

You love flirty embroidered slip dresses with shoestring shoulder straps, hand-crafted jewellery and the prettiest, flimsiest sandals. Cascading pre-Raphaelite curls or long, straight, modern-day-hippie hair are you. You rag-roll your hair to create tousled waves, and occasionally use heated rollers or tongs for the ultimate mane. Leave the ringlets after tonging, rather than brushing them out.

the femme fatale

Your clothes are often figure-hugging, low-cut, and designed to ensure that you turn heads wherever you go. Glamour is key. You adore vampy red lipstick and dramatic black eyeliner. You would never leave the house without a full face of make-up and you always wear nail polish, which is never chipped. Your hair – like the rest of you – is perfectly styled, and you often pile it on top of your head to create an air of studied casualness.

the party girl

Life is one big party. You love clothes that make an impact – anything glittery or sparkly will do. You'll wear your hair up or down, depending on your mood, and you love to experiment with the latest hair clips and accessories. Party girls are addicted to perfumed hairsprays, which are spritzed onto the hair before styling. The formulas containing lemon, ylang ylang or petitgrain essential oils help combat the effect of a smoky atmosphere.

the modernist

You wear minimalist tailoring in grey or black, neat dresses and poloneck sweaters with clean lines. If you wear any jewellery at all, it is likely to be simple, contemporary and made of silver. You prefer your face to be virtually bare of make-up – or at least to look as though it is. You hair is always cut in the style of the moment, perhaps a sleek, sharp cut with an asymmetric outline or an extra-short fringe. Fussiness of any kind is not for you.

the avant-gardist

The contents of your wardrobe reflects your rejection of established trends; you prefer to eschew the norm and define your own style. Your make-up and hair colour tend towards the extreme; your cut may be punky, and wax and pomade are your favourite styling products because they can be used to sculpt the hair to dramatic effect.

make-up

Far more than a device to simply enhance your appearance, make-up is now an integral part of your skincare regime. Foundations, powders, blushers, eyeshadows and lipsticks all contain ingredients designed to actively improve the condition of the skin while protecting it from the elements.

'What is Elegance? It is a sort of harmony that resembles beauty with the difference that the latter is more often a gift of nature and the former the result of art.'

Geneviève Antoine Dariaux, *Elegance*

Make-up is as much about expressing a feeling and attitude as it is about the products you use. It can be applied to accentuate the features you like and disguise those you dislike, or to create a totally new image. Just as paint, manipulated by an artist, brings colour and light to a landscape and its figures, make-up can add life and vitality to your complexion.

If you are aiming for a super-natural look, work with the earthy tones of nature – burnt sienna, mushroom, ochre, moss – to put together a flattering palette that will ensure you look like you – only better. Super-sheer textures give a hint of colour to the skin – a healthy glow rather than a deep tan; the closer the shade is to your skin tone, the more natural it will look.

A new generation of intelligent make-up formulas contain nature-derived molecules that are able to react to the environment. For instance, damaging ultraviolet light can be absorbed by 'photochromatic' or light-sensitive molecules and converted into a different type of energy that speeds up cell renewal. Seaweed extracts in foundations and powders actively regulate the production of sebum, while lipsticks can release extra colour throughout the day, triggered by the movements of the mouth. Sun filters in lipsticks provide a year-round shield against ultraviolet rays, while vitamins B and E will strengthen skin, lips and lashes and disarm ageing free radicals.

The notion that an application of base dusted with powder should create a canvas onto which you paint your features has been swept away and replaced by the new beauty ethic. This says that your skin should look like your own, only smoother and with fewer imperfections.

Foundations that will help your skin to look dewy, fresh and healthy are the beauty world's new Holy Grail. The trend towards glossy, gleaming skin means that a shiny complexion is to be actively pursued instead of kept at bay.

When the skin has a sheen, rather than a matte surface, it looks younger. This is because young skin has a naturally smooth surface that reflects the light well. Lotions – also known as primers – are generally applied before a base, while shine sticks are applied over foundation; both are effective ways of creating the illusion of freshness and vitality.

The best places to apply luminizer is high on the cheekbones, directly under the eyes and on the temples.

foundation

Foundations come in myriad forms and textures, from extremely fine finishes to thick and covering. Tinted moisturizers, liquid foundations, stick foundations and compact foundations are all available in moisturizing, semi-matte and oil-free bases. Some will include anti-pollution complexes and light-reflective particles to help the skin look younger and more radiant. Traditional compact foundations used to provide a more generous coverage, but many new formulations are comprised of water-based gels – some consisting of as much as 50 per cent water. These bases feel very fresh when you apply them and the water evaporates to leave a velvety, oil-free finish.

For daytime, foundation should exactly match the tone of your skin and should allow some of its texture to show through. The aim is to even out the appearance of the skin, not create a mask. Choose a foundation that is as sheer as you can get away with; a liquid base, rather than a compact foundation, will probably be suitable. Since contemporary bases are also treatments that can improve the condition of your skin, you should pick one that has an affinity with your skin type and its needs.

Night time is when you can confound some of the rules and discover how much foundation can change your look. You don't have to switch to a base that gives you more coverage. In fact, you can go for minimal base, maximum skin show-through and shine. Or, try using make-up that is more matte than you would wear in the day, but bear in mind that a totally matte base can make the skin look flat and you will need to spend more time creating contour and shape – although some matte bases contain illuminating micro-pigments that counteract the dulling effect. Start with a demi-matte base – the idea is that once powder is dusted on top and definition is added to the cheeks and eyes, you will look groomed and glamorous but not heavily made-up. Compact foundations are easy to touch up during the evening. They can be applied with a make-up brush for a natural finish, or with a sponge for a fuller, more covering finish. Many bases contain ingredients that are flexible – like Lycra for your skin – and so are resistant to settling into creases and wrinkles.

finding a base

Before buying, you should sample at least three bases, applying stripes of each shade at an angle to your jaw line. Leave the colour for 10 minutes or longer, then check the results in good daylight. The base that disappears on your skin is the shade for you. If you can't get an exact match, you may be able to create the right colour by mixing two bases together.

application

When make-up artists create a natural look they only apply base where the skin needs it – probably around the nose and cheeks where pores tend to be more noticeable. Some visagistes blend foundation with a firm paintbrush or eyeshadow brush, but many prefer to use their fingers because the warmth makes blending easier, enabling them to create a true 'second skin'. They almost always work with downward strokes, in the direction in which the facial hairs lie, because this gives a smoother finish.

For mere mortals, there is the foundation sponge, which can be used dry to give more coverage or slightly damp for a sheer finish. Run the sponge under warm water, then squeeze it out well in a clean towel. The water will thin the foundation slightly, making it easier to apply and blend. Angled sponges will help you to apply base to the corners of the nose and blend it in areas where there are lines or wrinkles. You may find that a firmer sponge is easier to use than a soft sponge because it will give you more control.

Apply foundation in good daylight, dabbing a small amount onto the forehead, nose, centre of the cheeks and the chin. Then work it towards, but not into, the hairline. Build foundation up gradually, applying a second coat to needy areas.

concealer

Concealer can be used to cover up and disguise all manner of blemishes from dark circles to spots. To lighten dark under-eye shadows, you can either use a paler shade of foundation than you have used on the rest of your face, or a purpose-made concealer. These provide more coverage than foundation since they contain more pigment, but it is important to find one that is not too heavy in texture so that it doesn't settle into the fine lines under your eyes. A light-reflecting concealer is especially good, and can also be used around the sides of the nose and where lines develop that run between the nose and mouth. Concealer is also useful for hiding the fine, purple veins on the eyelids, at the same time providing a base that will hold your eye make-up in place for longer. However, they should be applied very sparingly. Choose a very liquid concealer, perhaps one that is delivered via a pump-action brush or one that comes with a sponge applicator. Otherwise, using a small, firm eyeshadow or lip brush to apply concealer will give the best result. You should also check that your concealer is only slightly lighter than your foundation to avoid the panda-eye effect.

A heavier formula is appropriate for concealing spots. Look for one that is designed for the purpose as it will be oil-free and will contain healing and antibacterial ingredients.

powder

There are women who wouldn't dream of leaving the house without face powder and women who never use it. The fact is, however, that your choice of powder is just as important as the foundation you use. Powder will hold your foundation in place and can do a great deal to improve the appearance of your skin, giving it a more flawless finish.

Loose powder is the powder of choice for setting your foundation at the start of the day or evening. A compact powder will not give as fine a finish and is best saved for retouching make-up later. Some powders are milled to be much finer than others and these are the most desirable. Before you apply the brush to your face, dust any excess powder onto the back of your hand.

Colour choice is crucial, too. Many women go for the safe option of a translucent powder, but a tinted powder can often enhance the complexion more. A honey colour, for instance, might warm up your complexion without looking fake. You can also experiment creating different effects with powders of various shades. For example, a shade that is very slightly darker than your regular powder and foundation can be used to slim down a round face, a heavy jaw or a wide nose.

Sheen-boosting powders are also available and are especially good for evening. They make the skin look shiny rather than greasy and will hold your foundation in place.

bronzing powder

When you haven't seen the sun in months, bronzing powder is a beauty blessing. Take a large powder brush, swirl a little colour onto it and lightly dust off any excess. Then touch it onto areas of the face where the sun would naturally tan you first – the forehead, the cheekbones, the nose and chin. Take the colour down onto the neck and the cleavage.

Bronzing powders are available in a range of shades and finishes, some matte, some sparkly. The latter tend to look better on younger skins. For the most natural look, always use a shade that is not too dark or too orange. You could also try a sienna or brown-toned blusher as a bronzing powder.

Bronzing gels and lotions are also available and these need to be applied to well-moisturized skin so that dry areas don't 'grab' extra colour.

blusher

Blusher has the ability to transform your face. Depending on how you apply it and the shades you use, you can appear innocent or sophisticated in an instant.

Powder blush is the longest lasting but the most difficult to apply. The key is to build it up gradually using a big soft brush and remember that less is more. Skin-toned colours are the easiest to apply, but hotter shades like red and orange can look dramatic provided the texture is very sheer.

Cream and gel blushers give a fresh flush to the skin and look the most natural, but they don't last as well as powder blusher, especially on oily skin.

Matching your blusher to your lipstick is an essential beauty trick. If you are a woman who likes to change your lipstick colour with your wardrobe and your mood, then you are going to require a mini wardrobe of blusher colours, too. As a general rule, pale pink blushers look good on very pale, Scandinavian blondes; vivid pinks, reds and purples are great on black complexions; honey and caramel, peach and reddy-browns will suit redheads; and rosy-browns are good on brunettes.

shaping up

The principles of trompe l'oeil are helpful when shaping your face. Pale colours attract the light and so accentuate the features, while darker colours hollow and sculpt the face.

If you want to make a long, narrow face look fuller, use a paler shade of blusher and concentrate the colour on the area from the centre of the cheek to the outer edge of the eye.

For a modern edge, apply blusher very high on the cheekbones, almost directly under the eyes.

To slim down a round face, choose a medium to dark shade, suck in the cheeks and apply the blusher from just outside the centre of the cheeks up towards the hairline (but not into it). Avoid applying colour to the apples of the cheeks.

For a baby-faced flush, use colour on the apples of the cheeks only. Applying a cream or gel blusher with the fingers works well. Or use a round blusher brush, smile and apply colour with a circling motion. You can use a slightly brighter colour than you would usually use so that you look as though you have just returned from a country hike.

the brows

Leaving your brows *au naturel* is perfectly in tune with a fresh-faced look, but for a more made-up, polished appearance, your eye make-up should start with your eyebrows – they can make a much greater impact on your look than you may have realized. In fact, during any professional make-up lesson, considerable time will be spent shaping and shading the brows.

The line of the brows should form a gentle, sweeping curve, starting at the top of the nose and finishing at an imaginary diagonal line that leads from the centre of the mouth to the outside edge of the eye. Hold a pen straight up along the side of your nose to your brow to find the point where your eyebrow should begin. Then place the pen diagonally across your face from the centre of your mouth to the outer edge of your eye to see where it should finish. Pluck the brows from underneath, following the direction of growth of the hair. The shape of the brows will be determined firstly by your personal choice and the shape of your features and your eyes, and secondly by the dictates of fashion. Models and actresses may pluck above the brow line but this can lead to straggly brows and stronger growth and is generally advised against.

Grooming the brows should be done daily using an eyebrow comb or an old toothbrush with sweeping, upward strokes. You should always groom the brows before you apply pencil.

Buy an eyebrow pencil in a colour that exactly matches your natural brow colour or is no more than one shade darker. (Some women have their eyebrows lightened or coloured to tone in with their hair, a technique best performed by professional therapists.) Sharpen the pencil to a fine point so that you can draw very fine lines, and apply it using upward, sweeping lines to lengthen the face or horizontal lines to broaden the face.

Eyebrow shadows are quick to use and are also applied by making small strokes using the stiff, angled brush supplied. If you simply want to define your brows but don't need to extend the length or change the shape, a brow mascara is the simplest solution because it can be swept just once along the brow.

After applying eyebrow pencil or shadow, hold your brows in place by sweeping on eyebrow gel or by spraying a toothbrush with a little hairspray before touching it onto the brows.

If your brows are long and straggly, brush them upwards and use a pair of nail scissors to trim them slightly.

the eyes

You may prefer to apply eyeliner to both lids, or to the top or bottom lids only, but avoid joining it at the inner and outer edges as this closes up the eyes. Liquid eyeliners are most difficult to apply; pencils and shadows are easier because they can be blended. To apply liquid eyeliner, start at the inner corner of the eye, resting your drawing hand against your face and supporting the elbow in the palm of your other hand. To avoid hard lines, try applying a line of dark grey, navy, brown or black eyeshadow using a very stiff, flat brush. Simply press the tip of the brush onto the shadow at a 90 degree angle, then press the brush immediately below or above the lashes, repeating the movement along the lash line. Blend the line slightly with a pointed sponge applicator, cotton bud or soft, pointed brush.

Who'd leave home without mascara? There are mascaras just for definition, or you can double the impact with a lash-building mascara. For maximum thickness, look for a lash primer that will give a conditioning undercoat, or use a touch of Vaseline. Some mascaras lift the lashes slightly and open up the eyes. Lash curlers are difficult to master and need a confident hand; ask a beauty therapist to show you how. Eyelash perming is very effective, but should be done by a trained therapist.

The most effective way to apply mascara is by looking down into a mirror and gently lifting the top eyelid. Sweep down the lashes, then sweep up from the underside of the lashes to open the eyes. Leave to dry for a minute, then repeat if you wish. Avoid applying mascara to the lower lashes during the day so you don't look too made-up, and apply it only to the outer lower lashes for evening to avoid looking sad.

If you are nervous of applying eyeshadow, don't use one that is too heavy in colour and texture. An ultra-fine, silky shadow or cream will glide on and look so sheer that only a hint of colour is apparent. Subtle definition is best achieved with a make-up brush if you are using a shadow, as sponge applicators tend to give a more intense effect. Creams are a cinch to use as they are applied with the wand and then blended using the fingers.

Small eyes look bigger if you use pale mascara and pastel shadow – for instance, a slightly sparkly shadow with a hint of blue, green or lavender. Glossy gels and creams in light shades make the eyes look brighter.

Open up close-set eyes by using a lighter colour in the inner corners of the upper and/or lower lids; wide-set eyes need a darker shadow.

Deep-set eyes look strongest when you define them with eyeliner and apply one colour all over the lid up to the brow.

the lips

Lips should be plump and well moisturized, and you will find that they respond quickly to a little extra care and attention. Lips have no protective pigment of their own, so during the day wear a lipstick that contains ultraviolet filters; a lip block is essential if you are sunbathing or skiing. Look for lipsticks that contain anti-ageing vitamins A and E, nourishing shea butter and UVA/UVB filters. Remove any dry, flaky skin by rubbing the lips very gently with a wet toothbrush. Then apply a lip cream formulated for the job. If you don't have a specialist lip salve, apply a thick coat of moisturizer and leave it to be absorbed.

Lip pencil is a beauty life-saver when fine lines start to develop around the perimeter of the lips and cause lipstick to fray. It can also be used to change the shape of the lips, to give definition and to hold lipstick onto the lips for longer. Use a shade that is the same, or very close to, the colour of your lipstick. Nude lip pencils are also useful if you find that your lipstick wears off quickly – you may also like to try a moisturizing lip base that helps lock colour onto the lips. A lip pencil is far from essential and you may prefer to apply lipstick using a lip brush to create the shape you like and to give the lips a more natural look.

The texture of the lipstick and lip gloss you use and how you apply it creates dramatically different effects and can actually alter the shape of the mouth. A translucent stain looks healthy and sensual, while a more vivid, matte hue can be a power statement. Take a little lipstick onto your finger and dab it onto the lips, then blend it to give just a stain of colour. For the same effect, use a lip brush and blot the colour with a tissue. For a slightly fuller look with more colour, apply one coat of a creamy lipstick from the tube or with a brush. For the most dramatic effect, use lip pencil to define the outline of the lips and to fill them in. Then apply lipstick with a lip brush, blot it with a tissue, reapply and seal by pressing on a tiny amount of powder. Long-lasting lipstick, which takes a short time to set on the lips, can be very drying and you may need to apply lip balm once it has been removed. For the evening, a shimmering lip gloss that contains golden flecks will look super-glamorous, but remember that applying a gloss over a long-lasting lipstick will reduce the holding power. Instead, you may prefer a metallic lipstick as a night-long option. However, coloured lip glosses that contain longer-lasting pigments are increasingly available.

To make thin lips look fuller, apply lip pencil fractionally outside the line of the lips and use a paler, glossy lipstick.

For overfull lips, run lip pencil just inside the lip line and use dark lipsticks in matte finishes, or apply powder on top of a glossy lipstick to matte it down.

If your lips slant downwards, lift the edges of the mouth as you apply lip pencil to the corners.

make-up looks

Are you a fresh-faced outdoor girl with no more than a healthy returned-from-a-run glow to your cheeks? An outrageous vamp with come-to-bed eyes and glossy red lips? An oh-so-cute sex kitten with Bambi lashes and a kissable sugar-pink mouth? ...

The make-up you wear reveals a great deal about your personality and mood, and a change of colour and texture can dramatically alter your appearance. Go for all-over shine with a dewy, translucent complexion, or try a more polished look with a sophisticated matte finish. Eyes may be understated and natural with just a slick of mascara and highlighter, or they may be made-up for high drama with groomed brows, sultry eyeliner and smoky shadow. The simplest way to transform your face in an instant is with lipstick – go for sumptuous cherry-red, sexy burgundy or frosted baby-pink; dab on some gloss for extra poutiness and glamour. Alternatively, just give lips a barely-there stain and keep them moisturized with lip balm.

angel face

Floaty, light-as-air dresses flutter in your all-white bedroom. Your bed is scattered with lace pillows on an antique floral quilt. Novels by Gabriel García Márquez and Jean Giono are on your bedside table. Friends say you are a dreamer and a romantic, which of course you are. Needless to say, you believe in angels and spirits.

White iridescent eyeshadows and the prettiest fairy pink and lilac lipsticks are poetry in motion for you. You like the way they create an eye-catching kaleidoscope of colours as you turn your head. You have discovered myriad ways to make them modern. Sometimes you wear shadow on your upper lids only, at other times you will circle your eyes with it. Brows and lashes are left almost natural. Sometimes lipstick is applied just to the centre of the top and bottom lips.

For the evening, you love face powders and shine sticks that have a soft, ethereal sparkle. Your blush is a baby-pink powder and you might dust a little under the brows as well.

golden girl

A year-round tan – from a bottle, of course – is essential for your wellbeing; pale and interesting is a not a look you go for. Eighteen-carat gold enhances every complexion that already has a natural glow to it, and although it can look garish on paler skins, make-up in shades of gold is perfectly at home on your warm skin tones.

The sure way to make gold work is to use it to play up one area of the face predominantly – for instance, the eyes. Apply a little lustrous eyeshadow or cream to the outer brow bone only, then use a bronzing powder that has a subtle glimmer as blush. Lips, too, need a slight sparkle. You can either use a lipstick that already contains golden highlights, or mix the tiniest amount of golden eyeshadow with your lipstick and apply it with a brush.

Complete the look with a body lotion that contains particles of gold that will flicker in candlelight.

flower child

Your style is highly individual and bohemian, with printed or woven skirts, tie-front tops and braided hair. This hippie look is a style that takes imagination and creative flair to achieve.

Your fresh-faced beauty starts with gleaming skin – your complexion looks as though you have just stepped out of the shower and depends on a daily cleansing routine that lifts away the dead surface layer of cells, plus a twice-weekly exfoliating mask. Moisturizer gives your skin a dewy glow and you rarely use much powder.

A creamy blush on the apple of the cheeks gives you a rosy, flushed appearance. Smile and generously apply the colour in the middle of your cheeks directly below the centre of the eye using your fingers or a make-up sponge.

A translucent lip stain in a colour that is slightly brighter than your natural lip colour can be created in two ways. Either apply a rose-tinted lipstick with your finger, gently pressing it on – the idea is that the texture and tone of your own lips should still show through the colour – or use a tinted lip gloss and blot it well.

Your eyes are played down, with just a touch of a sandy or earthy shadow to emphasize the shape of your eyes and a brown or dark brown mascara, which is carefully combed through so that the lashes look as real as possible.

debutante

You are going to a ball this evening and will be wearing a long, asymmetric black dress. You'll have simple diamond studs in your ears and, on your wrists, an evening watch lent to you by your mother and the diamond bracelet you inherited from your aunt.

You have your hair dressed at a salon and your nails manicured and painted to match your lipstick. You want a classic make-up that is sophisticated and elegant. An alabaster complexion is going to be your canvas and you choose a semi-matte foundation that gives plenty of coverage, applying it with a slightly damp make-up sponge. Loose powder in a matching colour is pressed on top. You lightly define your brows with a pencil that is the same shade as your hair and brush them up with a brow brush.

A fine slick of dark brown eyeshadow is used to line the top lid, applied wet with a small eye-lining brush. Eyeshadows have a silky, not-too-matte-not-too-sparkly finish to them. Sand goes on the eyelid up to the crease and a rich brown is lightly applied above it. Black-brown thickening mascara is carefully combed through the lashes on each application.

A plum powder blush is applied sparingly to the cheeks and a matching deep wine, long-lasting lipstick slicked onto the lips, with just a touch of gloss in the centre of the lower lip.

rising star

You love to be noticed and play the femme fatale – dance floors are for dancing on, champagne is to be drunk ... You would save up for a month to buy the most exquisite dress that no-one else has – or use your credit card without hesitation. You don't flinch at sleeping in foam curlers every night in order to have Rapunzel's cascading waves in the morning.

You wouldn't dream of covering your freckles, so choose a super-sheer make-up and a fine, translucent powder. For a party, you'll highlight your cheeks with a smattering of glitter gel. You concentrate on making your eyes look bigger by applying a brighter colour underneath your eyes in a shade that reflects the golden flecks in your eyes.

A shimmering copper blush is teamed with a buff-coloured, moisturizing lipstick. You like your lips to look super-glossy, so you slick a long-lasting lip gleam on top.

As any cosmetics junkie will tell you, make-up can be great fun, so enjoy trying out new trends and seeing how different colours and textures transform your look.

make-up facts & tips

Use a small brush, such as a clean lip brush, to blend foundation to the base of the eyelashes, the inner and outer edges of the eyes, the brows and the sides of the nose.

Beware of using tinted green moisturizers or foundations to tone down redness – if the texture of the product is too heavy, you may end up with a green cast to your complexion which is not attractive!

Revolutionary technology means that you can have a base that looks as though you've just applied it – all day long. The silicone in the new formulations evaporates within a minute, leaving the colour locked onto your skin, yet feeling comfortable hour after hour.

Look out for make-up fixing sprays which coat the complexion with a long-lasting, invisible film.

When applying make-up, remember that lighter colours will make features look larger, and darker colours will help an area to recede.

Coloured mascaras can greatly enhance certain eye colours – maroon or purple mascara will bring out the colour of blue or green eyes, while black, charcoal or dark brown moiré mascaras that have a touch of iridescence, such as silver or gold tones, can highlight hazel or dark brown eyes.

When you are correcting the shape of the lips, you can apply a little concealer before you redraw the outline. Concealer will also help thin lips to appear more prominent.

Darker shades of lipstick require a lip brush to apply them. A brush will also help you to layer the colour onto the lips for a longer-lasting result.

To create a well-defined lip contour on wrinkled lips, smile before applying lip pencil and lipstick.

Avoid oily food if you want your lipstick to last.

Bear in mind that pale, glossy shades of lipstick will make thin or small lips look larger, while dark shades will make them look even smaller.

You can use concealer to help thin lips appear more prominent. Apply a little concealer around the lip line before you redraw a new outline.

If you don't have time for a weekly manicure, apply cuticle oil every night to strengthen the nails and wear pale, low-maintenance shades.

Keep a white eye pencil in your make-up bag and apply it to the inner corner of the eyes when you are tired or when your eyes are red.

Consider making one feature your beauty trademark – you could wear liquid eyeliner, bright lipstick or an eye-catching nail polish each day.

fragrance

Fragrance is the ultimate mood-booster with the ability to trigger powerful memories and emotions. It enhances our wellbeing and is a potent means of personal expression. As well as wearing scent, there are endless ways to release it into your home, including sprays, candles, vaporizers and incense.

'Under the heat and sun, leaves and flowers store up their scents, which are later released by darkness, cool air and dew. In the evenings, the gardens float amid clouds of scent. Eucalyptus and cypress give off delicious fragrances. Then come the roses and the jasmines of the famous hills of Grasse, where many well-known perfumers have made their homes.'

Marie-Françoise Valery, *Gardens of Provence and the Côte d'Azur*

To talk about perfume is to talk about passion, since it is, of course, the ultimate sensory experience and also a highly sensual one. The smell of a baby's skin, your mother's perfume as she kisses you goodnight, your lover's unique scent lingering in your bed, the heady aroma of a field of lavender or a rose garden in summer – these are the things that we remember with the passing years and that instantly have the power to conjure up forgotten memories, re-create emotions and transport us to a different time and place.

Scents travel directly to a part of the brain's limbic system that is situated immediately above the nose, called the olfactory bulb. According to Dr Steve Van Toller of the University of Warwick's Department of Psychology, England, it is a fundamental part of the brain that was present in prehistoric animals. In the human brain, the limbic system is associated with our sense of smell, basic emotions, memory, sexual feelings and learning. Recent work by Dr Van Toller has shown that babies are able to smell even when they are still in the womb. 'We know that they would smell tobacco in the bloodstream if the mother smoked and ate food like curry,' he says.

Despite its ability to enhance our lives – for its own value, because of its effects on our other senses and because of the associations it recalls to mind – our sense of smell is something we often take for granted and forget to use. Yet it can greatly enhance the experiences we have. For example, wine tastes completely different when it is served in a large glass and you deeply inhale the aroma before sipping it. When you consciously start to use your nose and learn to identify individual aromas, as a perfumer does, it will open up a whole new world.

Fragrance is unquestionably a secret, seductive weapon that can be used to dramatic effect. Aromatherapy expert Valerie Ann Worwood recommends a process she calls the memory imprint method. 'When you are wearing a new fragrance, note whether your partner comments favourably and, provided the first time you wore it was an enjoyable time, you should apply the fragrance again on five consecutive occasions. After that, your fragrance will be imprinted on your partner's mind forever and, whenever he smells it, he will think immediately of you.'

'There was a woman I felt very passionate about. I don't see her any more but whenever I smell her fragrance, waves of emotions sweep over me,' confessed a male friend recently.

Everyone has a unique natural body scent which plays a large role in our attractiveness – or otherwise – to others. In his book, *The Romantic Story of Scent*, John Trueman explains how personal aromas play a key part in human love. 'When we kiss we are performing an attenuated ceremony of greeting by smelling; in many primitive languages the word for kiss or greet is the same as that for smell. Nonetheless, we would probably quickly be turned off if our loved one whispered "I want to be smelled" rather than "I want to be kissed".' He also writes that the unique smell of every woman varies according to the colour of her hair. Redheads have the strongest body scent, which is reminiscent of amber or violets, brunettes smell of ebony and blondes smell more subtly of amber or violets.

In her book, *Miller's Perfume Bottles – A Collector's Guide*, Madeleine Marsh explains the history of scent. Many ancient civilizations used to burn aromatic substances in the temples to please the gods and to mask the smell of burning flesh that resulted from sacrifices – the word perfume comes from the Latin *per fumum*, meaning 'through smoke'. Thousands of years later, incense is still part of religious rituals in many parts of the world. The Emperor Nero was hugely extravagant in his use of perfume. On one infamous occasion he spent the equivalent of £100,000 on a waterfall of rose petals that smothered and killed one of his guests. In ancient Egypt, too, flower extracts and essences were widely used in all aspects of life – to fragrance bath water, anoint the hair and body, and to scent homes and temples. Fragrance was also part of the ritual of mummification – corpses were embalmed with myrrh and cassia and then wrapped up in scented bandages.

When the Roman Empire collapsed, the use of perfume for pleasure was discouraged. It was not until the Crusaders returned from the East with a variety of new spices and ointments that the art of perfumery flourished again in Western courts, and essences were imported for use in perfumery and medicine.

'Scents are surer than sights and sounds to make your heart-strings crack.'

Rudyard Kipling

fragrant themes

Fragrances are classified by families and some can be deemed to belong to more than one family. In her book, *Perfume*, fragrance expert Susan Irvine explains the different types of scents and points out that understanding the family traits will help to guide you towards the type of scent you will probably like at the fragrance counter.

florals

This is the largest fragrance category, within which there are key family units.

Aldehydic florals were introduced in 1921 with Chanel No. 5, which uses them to great effect along with jasmine absolute from Grasse. Aldehydes are synthetic notes that are used to enhance a fragrance's top notes – the first layer of scent that hits you initially – and to bring a 'champagne sparkle' to a fragrance. Women who want a modern yet sensual feeling from their fragrance are often aldehyde addicts.

Green florals are redolent of freshly cut grass and ivy leaves. Green fragrance fans include women who like a sharp fragrance with an assertive air.

Fruity florals include a range of fruit notes, from passion fruit to apples. If you have a vivacious personality, these fragrances are for you.

Fresh florals include clean, transparent flower notes or citrus notes. Women who like their fragrance to smell light and natural feel most at home with fresh florals as part of their fragrance wardrobes.

Woody florals feature woody notes in the base of the fragrance. These are for the woman with an adventurous spirit and a love of wide open spaces and the great outdoors.

Sweet florals have exotic or intense floral notes predominating. Sweet floral aficionados will often hide their passion.

chypres

Strong, spicy and slightly powdery, these fragrances are based on the contrast between bergamot-type top notes and mossy base notes.

It was Coty's Chypre of 1917, with orange, geranium, spices and oakmoss, that inspired a whole new family of perfumes.

These scents are for strong women who like to be provocative.

ozonic

Ozonic notes give a fragrance the tingling freshness of a light sea breeze.

Originally, ozonic notes were added to detergents to give them a clean, bright, refreshing smell.

Ozonics are now one of the leading fragrance categories and they are often added to light floral notes and warm bases for a scent that takes you back to holidays on the seashore under a hot sun.

Anyone who is looking for an uplifting, light and summery scent will like to wear this type of fragrance.

orientals

This fragrance family, known by the French as *ambre*, meaning amber, are musky, spicy and voluptuous.

Within this category are two key subdivisions, the florientals and the spicy orientals.

Pepper, aniseed and cardamom are some of the ingredients that are spicing up the latest sensual, fragrant offerings. The combination of chocolate, vanilla and dewberry is another mouthwatering, addictive mix.

If you like to experience life in all its intensities and people find you enigmatic and mysterious, the orientals will appeal to you.

fougères

The overall impression of a fougère is of a fresh, woodland scent, often with lavender-accented top notes with a touch of coumarin, which is the smell of freshly cut hay.

Fougères is French for fern, although in reality ferns have no distinct fragrance.

Michael Edwards explains in *Perfume Legends* that Houbigant's Fougère Royale in 1882 pioneered the use of synthetic raw materials in perfumery, but Jicky is regarded as the first modern perfume because it was the first sophisticated composition. Before Jicky, perfumes had been made with a single floral note.

There are different categories of fougères, but in general, those who like them tend to be avant-garde.

'For a moment he was so confused that he actually thought he had never in all his life seen anything so beautiful as this girl ... He meant, of course, he had never smelled anything so beautiful.'

Patrick Suskind, *Perfume*

the fine art of wearing fragrance

Next time you reach for your favourite fragrance, stop for a moment to think about how you wear it. Most people tend to apply a touch of eau de toilette – the least concentrated form of scent – to their wrists or behind their ears and wonder why it doesn't last. Yet eau de toilette was originally created simply to wake us up or to refresh us. It is formulated to be sprayed all over the body, while perfume, which is much longer-lasting, should be applied to pulse points – but not behind the ears where there are too many sebaceous glands, which can affect the way a perfume smells. Perfume, available as a liquid or concentrated solid, is especially effective when applied to the collarbone, while eau de toilette can be sprayed into the hair so that you smell your fragrance whenever you turn your head.

When you buy a new scent, you are not just faced with a baffling array of smells from which to choose. These days, the packaging is arguably as much of an art form as the concoction of the fragrance it contains, with beautiful bottles and atomizers in all shapes, sizes and colours that would grace any dressing table. However alluring these may be, let your nose, rather than your eye, make the final choice.

A good perfume will fuel your fantasies and even has the ability to create a new personality for the wearer, tapping into the alter ego.

The majority of fragrances are constructed with a harmony of top, middle and base notes, the combination of which gives a scent its unique character and depth. These notes, or layers, of fragrance often belong to different fragrance families and, although they complement each other, they often have quite different smells. It is important, therefore, to make sure that you still like the scent while it changes considerably over a period of hours, as one note fades and is replaced by another.

When you first apply a fragrance, the top note, which is often the lightest and freshest in character, is what you smell initially. This lasts for the shortest time before fading to the middle note and, finally, the base note, which is

usually a deeper and more lingering scent. If a fragrance smells overpowering, this indicates either that it contains a lot of synthetic ingredients or that you are merely smelling the initial hit of alcohol, rather than the true, underlying scent. Classic eau de colognes, however, consist of single floral notes, while some of the newer scent introductions are lateral fragrances that maintain the same smell throughout the day.

In addition to the more traditional forms of fragrance - perfume, eau de toilette and eau de cologne - many perfume manufacturers produce a wide variety of bathing and body-care products within the same scent range, including bubble bath, body lotion and deodorant. Although purchasing the entire range may seem a pure indulgence, rather than a luxurious necessity, using a combination of these different products is a good way of layering your fragrance and ensuring that it lasts with you throughout the day. After bathing and applying the deodorant, spray yourself all over with the eau de toilette to freshen and tone your skin, then smooth on the softening body lotion. Finally, apply a little perfume to some of your pulse points. The perfume formulation is the smoothest and roundest of all the concentrations. It contains 20 to 40 per cent of the pure fragrance and is formulated with more of the stable fixatives, which is why it lasts so much longer. Perfume extract is over 50 per cent perfume concentrate.

Remember that using heavily perfumed commercial soaps or shampoos may clash with your fragrance.

natural extracts

Fragrances that contain large quantities of natural ingredients are some of the most sensual. The following combinations create quite different auras:

Mysterious Try concentrated rosewood with carnation, geranium and lavender.

Energetic Try cinnamon and orange, with the warmth of iris.

Warm and Sweet Try honeysuckle and ylang ylang, balanced with the green note of basil and ending with refreshing galbanum (extracted from a herbaceous plant).

Sensuous Try exotic jasmine, teamed with synthetic musk and almond kernel.

choosing fragrance

How can you tell if a fragrance really suits you and ensure that it lasts as long as you want it to?

Always use blotters, or smelling strips, when testing fragrances in a store. This method, which is favoured by perfumers, will enable you to smell a large number of fragrances without your sense of smell becoming exhausted.

If you apply fragrance to the skin, the warmth of your body gives the fragrance so much aura that you can only smell a few in one session.

John Oakes, perfume expert and author of *The Book of Perfumes*, recommends allowing a minute or so between smelling different scents and points out that you shouldn't rub a perfume once you have applied it or you will 'bruise' the ingredients.

Ideally, decide on two or three fragrances you like, then spray yourself with just one of them from a distance so that only the light vapour touches your skin.

Live with the fragrance for the rest of the day and if possible that night. Most women don't give themselves enough time when choosing a fragrance. Some perfume experts say that you only really know a fragrance when you have slept in it.

Return to the store and test your second fragrance on another day.

Remember that although you may like the smell of a scent on someone else, it may be completely different on you. A fragrance can vary depending on the pH of the skin.

Avoid testing a fragrance for several days if you have eaten spicy foods or garlic, unless these foods are a regular part of your diet.

Stress, medication and hormonal changes, such as menopause, can also affect how a fragrance smells on you.

home fragrance

Scenting the home is now a major force in interior design. It is a way of personalizing a living space that has become as important to many people as their colour scheme and the style of their furnishings.

creating moods

There are many versatile and ingenious ways in which you can introduce enticing scents into your surroundings to personalize your living space and create different moods. For instance, you can burn scented candles that release warm, inviting aromas and create a welcoming, flattering light when you're holding a party; you can sprinkle rosewater - a known relaxant and aphrodisiac - on your bed linen; or vaporize stimulating rosemary oil in your office to give your brain a boost while you're working.

Even a jar of nutmeg, a bundle of cinnamon, a bunch of fresh herbs or a vase of fragrant flowers, such as hyacinths, freesias, roses or lilies, can infuse the room with scent. Think of the wonderful, heady aromas that fill the air in an outdoor market on a warm day, where flower stalls are laden with lavender, roses and broom, herb and spice corners are filled with cinnamon, cardamom and rosemary, and food stalls are brimming with cheeses, fruit and vegetables, honey, nuts and candied fruit.

Once you are aware of the effect that fragrance can have on your mood, you will find that it opens up a whole new dimension for you to explore. Whether you like the idea of a row of fresh, fragrant herbs growing on your windowsill in rustic terracotta pots, a vase of old-fashioned blowsy roses beside your bed, an incense holder on your mantelpiece, scented candles by your bath, herb-filled sachets in your drawers and wardrobe or a bowl of amber resin on your desk, the following ideas and suggestions should give you a starting point from which to experiment. There are no hard and fast rules when it comes to the fragrances you choose or the methods your use to scent your home - the main thing is to surround yourself with smells that you enjoy and that have an uplifting effect on your spirits.

entertaining

The aim is to create an inviting atmosphere that puts people at ease and also stimulates and encourages conversation. Candles are a great choice for dinners or parties because the twinkling flames instantly create an intimate, magical light. Although you may want to use a quick burst of room spray to neutralize the smell of tobacco smoke or strong cooking odours, you shouldn't use anything that will clash with the food or is too overpowering. Try vanilla - a sweet, powdery note that rekindles childhood memories; refreshing, fruity aromas such as orange or mandarin; spicy notes of cinnamon or juniper; or warm and welcoming pine, cypress or thyme.

winding down

The pressure and pace of life in the twenty-first century can often be daunting and exhausting. Perhaps now more than ever, in a culture where people can, if they choose, be on the move all the time and in constant touch with family, friends and the office, it is essential to take time out to recharge your batteries and restore peace of mind.

Your home should be the one place to which you can retreat for ultimate relaxation. It should be a tranquil haven where you don't have to answer the phone or the doorbell unless you want to, but can simply rest your body and order your thoughts.

Proper relaxation is also the best way to ensure a good night's sleep. Since it often takes a while to switch off from the worries and preoccupations of the day, try to get into the habit of starting the process before you actually go to bed. Kick off your shoes and work clothes, make a soothing camomile tea or a milky drink, and settle down in a comfortable chair. Try burning candles or incense scented with relaxing fragrances such as melissa, sandalwood, ylang ylang, neroli or petitgrain to create a calming atmosphere. Breathe deeply to inhale the soothing vapours.

amber resin

Amber resin has a distinctive warm, sensuous, slightly spicy smell with hints of beeswax, vanilla and myrrh that instantly conjures up images of the Orient. Irregular cubes of this solid perfume are a lovely, natural way to introduce subtle fragrance to your home. They look attractive displayed in a simple bowl and can be mixed with a spice- or wood-based potpourri, placed inside a perforated perfume holder, or simply arranged among clothes in drawers and wardrobes. Amber resin cannot be burnt and should be kept out of the reach of children in case it is mistaken for sugar lumps.

incense

Incense is one of the most ancient methods of infusing scent into the surroundings and was often used in religious ceremonies because it helped to encourage meditation. Incense was so highly prized that a trade route was opened to transport it in large quantities from the East to the West.

For a long time the exclusive domain of hippies and New Age enthusiasts, incense is now back in fashion, providing an atmospheric way to scent your home. Many cutting-edge furnishing stores now sell incense holders and burners that are utterly in keeping with today's design-conscious interiors. Scented with a variety of delicious fragrances, traditional incense sticks or cones will burn for around 20 minutes and create a relaxing, dreamy atmosphere.

romantic liaisons

Perfume is key to the pleasure principle, since fragrance molecules, released by vaporizers or scented candles, travel straight to the limbic system where we process the experience of pleasure. There is a variety of exotic scents to choose from:

Cedar and juniper are woody fragrances that appeal to men particularly.

Rose is perhaps the ultimate scent for love and a traditional symbol of romance. For a truly voluptuous, contemporary scent, combine velvety rose with stimulating pepper.

Frankincense and myrrh are exotic, spicy and powdery. They can be blended to create a heady balsamic mix of vanilla, bergamot, sage and coriander – a potent combination!

vaporizing essences

Essential oils have been used for centuries for their aphrodisiac and relaxing properties. Romanic elixirs include benzoin, bergamot, geranium, jasmine, lavender, neroli, patchouli, rose and ylang ylang. Vaporizing essential oils is an easy way to create a romantic or passionate atmosphere in minutes. Place a little water in the well at the top of the vaporizer, then add 3 to 4 drops of your chosen oil and switch it on, if electric, or light the candle (do not leave a burning night-light or candle unattended). If you don't have a vaporizer, place a small bowl of hot water on top of a radiator and add the oils to that. You can also add drops of essential oil to the pool of hot, molten wax that forms around the burning wick of a standard pillar candle. Blow out the flame before you add the oil, then relight it. The heat will vaporize the essential oil molecules and release them into the atmosphere.

setting the scene

Piles of unwashed clothes or an unmade bed are not conducive to feeling relaxed and cosseted, whereas a seductively dressed bed, soft lighting and the pervading aroma of aphrodisiac oils can certainly put you in the mood for love!

You may want to create a true boudoir that is a shrine to your femininity, with plenty of lace, satin and floral fabrics, or you could consider decorating your bedroom with a rich, warm, more masculine palette. When it comes to bed linen, choose between pure cotton, sensual silk or satin, or crisp linen sheets. In the winter, top the bed with a soft, cuddly fleece or fake-fur throw for maximum tactility. If you are a true romantic, sprinkle rosewater on your sheets and scatter them with fragrant petals.

creative minds

Ditch the coffee – it will only give you the jitters and send your energy levels onto a roller-coaster ride – and switch on the vaporizer. When you are looking for inspiration or need to concentrate, essential oils are the stars of the show, since they work on the intellect via the spleen (which is the seat of our IQ), as well as directly affecting the mind and nervous system.

Ceramic rings for light bulbs are another good, easy way to release essential oils into the atmosphere. Simply place a few drops of oil onto the ring before you place it on top of a cold light bulb, then switch the lamp on. Essentials oils are flammable, so do not drop oil onto a ring that is sitting on top of warm bulb.

Aromatherapy expert Gabriel Mojay explains the properties of key oils for clearing the mind and easing furrowed brows in his book, *Aromatherapy for Healing the Spirit*:

Rosemary oil is one of the best-known oils for boosting concentration and memory. It helps to move energy upwards and so stimulates the brain's activity.

Tea tree oil is a nervous tonic, which is suitable if concentration is affected by poor vitality.

Cardamom and coriander seed enhance creativity and curiosity.

Marjoram and clary sage can increase clear thinking if you are tired and tense.

Lemon is one of the most effective oils if you are feeling muzzy-headed and dull. It can also improve learning.

Geranium and vetiver will help calm those who suffer from nervous anxiety and panic attacks.

Jasmine will help to lift depression, while ylang ylang will still a racing mind.

To ease stress symptoms, place 2 drops of lavender oil on a tissue and inhale.

Gabriel Mojay's Massage Blend

20 ml of carrier oil
3 drops clary sage essential oil
2 drops rosemary essential oil

home sweet home

Essential oils, many of which are antibacterial and antiseptic, can be used to clean the home instead of, or in addition to, chemical-laden products. When you are cleaning the fridge, freezer or oven, aromatherapist Valerie Worwood recommends adding 1 drop of lemon, or any of the other citrus oils such as grapefruit, lime, bergamot, orange or mandarin, to the water used for the final rinse. She also suggests applying 2 drops of eucalyptus oil to a damp cloth and using it to wipe down the surfaces. You can also add 2 drops of tea tree oil and 2 drops of lemon oil to a bucket of warm water and use it to clean surfaces and floors.

floral linen water

Scenting your clothes and bed linen with delicate floral fragrances is a great way to ensure that you are surrounded by an uplifting, natural perfume all the time. You can either buy a specially blended linen water or make your own by adding a drop of essential oil, such as rose, lavender or neroli, to a bottle of water. Pour it into a spritzer and spray a little onto your laundry before you iron it.

To help you drift off into a deep, soothing sleep, you can place some dried lavender or camomile flowers inside a cotton or muslin bag and slip it inside your pillowcase.

room fresheners

Ready-blended home fragrance spray, available in a wide variety of scents, including floral, citrus and spicy blends, is another instant way to refresh and scent your surroundings. It also helps mask the smell of tobacco smoke, pets or cooking. Simply spritz it into the air or spray it onto carpets, curtains or bed linen. Formulas that contain alcohol should not be used on fabrics that might fade.

You can mix your own room sprays by adding 2 drops of essential oil to 150 ml of warm water in a clean plant mister. Tea tree oil is antibacterial and antiviral, so it can be included in a room spray to reduce the spread of colds or flu. Use this mixture to wipe door handles and telephone receivers, too.

weekend plan

This is time for you; an opportunity to indulge yourself a little, to surrender body and soul to the pure pleasures of heavenly bath treatments and sensuous massage oils. You can treat your skin to a professional-style facial and energize your body with revitalizing essential oils. It's easy and it's mood-enhancing.

friday evening

Switch off from a long week and wind down for the weekend, calm your mind and forget your worries. Start by kicking off your shoes and playing some soothing music.

Prepare to do some gentle stretching. Emotional stress builds up in different muscles, and stretching will help to release the tension. (Feelings of anxiety afterwards indicate that your worries have been released, so sit quietly and become conscious of the sensations in your body; this may help you understand your concerns.) Warm up for a few minutes by walking around the room, swinging and circling your arms.

Begin with an upper-body stretch: bend your knees slightly and bend forwards from the waist, linking your hands together and stretching them away in front of you. Hold for 10–30 seconds and breathe deeply.

Stretch your hamstrings by placing the heel of your right foot on the ground in front of you with your leg straight. Bend the left knee and lean forward slightly over the right leg. Hold for 10–30 seconds and repeat on the other leg.

Retreat to the bathroom, light a scented candle – try calming, refreshing orange – and run a warm bath. Add 2–3 drops of mandarin and 2–3 drops of ylang ylang essential oils to boost flagging spirits and ease feeling of exhaustion. Swirl the water thoroughly before you step in and close the door to retain the aromas.

Use a loofah or body mitt on dry skin before you step into the bath to stimulate your circulation and help detox your system. Use long, sweeping movements, working towards the heart.

After a 20-minute soak, apply a sensual treat such as dry body oil, which can be sprayed all over to leave a light, fresh scent.

Make a soothing herbal tea – camomile will help you unwind.

Wrap up in a robe and lie on the sofa or bed. Place a lavender-filled eye pillow over your eyes and listen to your breathing. Picture yourself on a hillside. Imagine you have balloons with you that you can inflate. See yourself breathing your worries into each balloon in turn. Tie the ends, then release the balloons into the sky and watch them float away.

Prepare a nourishing supper of freshly pressed juice – try apple and pear or orange and carrot – and a warm chicken or tofu salad. Include baby salad leaves and follow it with fresh fruit, such as berries or melon.

Go to bed early. To aid sleep, add 1 drop of lavender oil to 2 ml of a carrier oil, such as sweet almond oil, and rub it into your shoulders, temples and the back of your neck.

saturday morning

Naturopathic physicians emphasize the importance of eating fresh foods and ensuring that you get outside into the fresh air and light every day. Follow these simple principles to help increase your energy levels. If you are planning an evening out, use the revitalizing bath oils.

Eat a breakfast of home-made muesli that is full of nuts, oats, wheatbran and raisons or currants. Add some fresh fruit, such as strawberries, raspberries, blueberries or melon, and top it with live yoghurt. Drink a herbal tea and one of your favourite blends of freshly squeezed juices for a boost of vitamin C.

Raise your energy levels by going for a brisk 15-minute walk or run; then have a relaxing swim to stretch out all your muscles

After your fitness session, have a steam bath or sauna to open and cleanse your pores.

Either dry-brush your skin before you shower or use a foaming body scrub, concentrating especially on extra-dry areas such as the knees, shins and elbows.

Apply a revitalizing massage oil all over your body. For instance, one that is already blended with invigorating peppermint, rosemary and pine. Massage your neck and shoulders firmly for several minutes.

Use a little pure shea butter to deeply moisturize your lips, elbows, knees and feet.

saturday afternoon/evening

Saturday night is the time to let your hair down and have fun. Whatever your plans, make sure you look your best and feel uplifted and full of vitality.

Have a warm bath scented with foaming bath salts that contain essentials oils, or add essential oils diluted in a tablespoon of carrier oil. For a calming, stress-relieving blend use 3 drops of ylang ylang, 2 drops of basil and 2 drops of mandarin oils. For an energizing mix, use 3 drops of grapefruit, 3 drops of lemon and 2 drops of lime oils.

Wash your hair with a shampoo tailored to your hair type and apply a deep-acting conditioner. If you have dry, damaged hair a mask will leave it soft and easy to handle. Add 5 drops of lavender, 4 drops of ylang ylang and 3 drops of camomile oils to 24 ml of apricot kernel carrier oil and apply it to the hair before shampooing. Leave it on for 5–10 minutes and rinse thoroughly.

Apply a rich body milk and handcream – look out for shea butter formulations for the softest-ever skin.

Give yourself a manicure and pedicure (see page 37). Use a pumice stone or a foot file on any hard skin on your feet, then exfoliate the whole foot using a foaming scrub gel or softening hand scrub. Always cut your toenails straight across in order to avoid in-growing nails.

sunday morning

The following tactics will pep you up and are especially effective if you stayed out late last night and over-indulged with rich food and alcohol.

Have a breakfast of sugar-free cereal, yoghurt, nuts, seeds and fruit.

Drink plenty of freshly squeezed orange juice or a citron pressé, which is a freshly squeezed lemon mixed half and half with water. This will help rehydrate you and replenish your body's supplies of vitamin C.

To help ease a hangover, take up to 3 g of vitamin C and 1 g of evening primrose oil, plus a B-complex vitamin after eating.

Use a ready-made eye mask that will help reduce puffiness; look for one containing soothing extracts of geranium, rose or camomile. Or, for a home-made compress, steep two round cotton-wool pads in cool cornflower or witch hazel and apply the pads to closed eyes for 5 minutes.

After brushing your skin and showering, apply a stimulating and detoxifying essential oil massage blend to your body. Add 4 drops of lemongrass, 3 drops of pine and 3 drops of lime oils to 30 ml of grapeseed or apricot kernel carrier oil and massage it into the skin with firm, circular movements.

Retreat to the bathroom and give yourself a 5-minute facial massage (see page 56).

Apply some make-up – it will make you feel better! Try out new colour combinations or stick to the super-natural look, which suits most skin types because it enhances the wearer's own tones, rather than contrasting with them. The shades for eyes, cheeks and lips are very similar and so complement each other:

Face: Apply your usual liquid foundation. Using a large blusher brush, sweep a touch of desert-rose blusher onto the apples of the cheeks. Finish with a dab of face powder, just where you need it.

Eyes: Blend a little frosted sienna eyeshadow onto the top eyelid, fading it out to finish just above the crease. Apply your favourite mascara and brush your brows up.

Lips: Using a lip brush, apply just a little desert-rose lipstick, leaving the natural skin colour to show through.

sunday evening

Prepare yourself mentally for the week ahead.

Take 15 minutes to reflect on your lifestyle and your goals. Light a soothing scented candle or incense stick and sit quietly with your eyes closed, focusing on your breathing. Allow any thoughts to come up to the surface of your conscious mind. Consider each one calmly and allow it to float away when it is ready. You may question whether your weekly schedule gives you enough opportunity for fun, relaxation, pastimes, exercise and for eating well.

Spritz your bedroom with a relaxing room spray – perhaps one containing lavender, neroli, ylang ylang or rose.

Go to bed early with a camomile tea or warm milky drink to aid sleep.

aromatherapy

Imagine having a cosmetics laboratory where you can mix your own natural products that lift your mood, enhance your physical and spiritual wellbeing, and improve the condition of your skin and hair. Aromatherapy, the science of essential oils, allows you to do this.

'All who know the pure product and use it with understanding come to respect the essential oils. One cannot but admire their ability to operate effectively not only on the cellular, physical level, but in the emotional, intellectual, spiritual and aesthetic areas of our lives also.'

Valerie Ann Worwood, *The Fragrant Pharmacy*

Essential oils are the life source of a plant. They are so concentrated that they are only ever used in dilution and in very small quantities. The oils are extracted from various parts of a plant – the flowers, leaves, stalks, stems, sap, wood, bark, nuts or berries.

There are two ways in which essential oils can enter the body – absorption and inhalation. The molecules are small enough to be absorbed directly through the skin and then into the bloodstream, by which means they are carried around the body, working on its nerves and organs. Essential oils are very volatile and vaporize easily when heat is applied to them. When the aromatic steam is inhaled, the molecules travel directly to the brain's limbic system. This is the very centre of our emotions, and different oils can have very different effects on our psyche.

The active properties of essential oils varies according to when and where the plant material was harvested and how the oils were extracted. Skilled extraction will ensure that the oil is pure and that its full strength, energy and potential is preserved. It is therefore advisable only to buy aromatherapy oils from a respected manufacturer. Oils of lesser quality, which have little or no therapeutic action, are used by the fragrance industry.

Oils are extracted from the raw plant material through a variety of methods. The oil in the rinds of citrus fruit, for example, is squeezed out under pressure in a relatively simple process called expression, whereas vacuum, steam and carbon dioxide distillation – more complex and costly processes – may be used for other flowers and herbs. Some plants, such as lavender, give up their precious oils more easily than others, making them less expensive than others. Neroli (orange blossom), jasmine and rose are some of the most expensive oils, since hundreds of kilos of the freshly picked blossom is needed to obtain the very potent and fragrant elixirs.

'These extremely complex precious liquids are extracted from very specific species of plant life and are in harmony with people and planet life.'

Valerie Ann Worwood, *The Fragrant Pharmacy*

how to use essential oils

In the Bath Add the recommended number of drops of essential oil (but no more than 10 in total) to 20 ml (one tablespoon) of neutral foam or vegetable oil and pour it under running water.
As a Massage Blend 10–12 drops of one or more essential oils into 30 ml of a carrier massage oil.
For a Facial Moisturizer Place 2 drops of essential oil in 4 ml of a neutral lotion or cream base. Avoid applying it near the eyes.
For a Body Lotion Place 5 drops of essential oil in 10 ml of a neutral lotion or cream base.
In a Sauna Add 3 or 4 drops of essential oil to a ladle of water and pour it over the hot coals.
In a Perfume Diffuser Also known as a vaporizer. Add 3 or 4 drops of essential oil to a little water in the dish before switching it on or lighting the candle underneath.
In a Room Spray Add 2 drops of essential oil to 150 ml of warm water in a clean plant mister.

When you are blending your own aromatherapy treats, look for bath and massage oils that combine skin-protective oils, such as nourishing grapeseed oil (widely recognized for its anti-ageing properties) and softening apricot kernel oil.

As well as mixing your own blends, you can also enjoy using ready-made essential oil-based candles, skincare and haircare products, soaps, foam baths, massage oils and bath salts.

dos and don'ts

Essential oils are damaged by heat, humidity and light, so must be stored in dark glass bottles. For best results, they should be used within two years of extraction, or one year in the case of citrus oils. The oils are extremely powerful and must be respected.

Essential oils are for external use only, unless prescribed otherwise by a qualified aromatherapist.

Never apply essential oil directly to the skin (except lavender oil, which can be used to soothe burns, insect bites and spots).

Do not let essential oils come into contact with the eyes; if this occurs, rinse thoroughly with milk or vegetable oil, then consult your doctor.

Skin should not be exposed to the sun after applying essential oils, especially citrus oils, as they accelerate the skin's reaction to the sun. Be aware that a number of oils can irritate or sensitize the skin.

Essential oils can build up in the body, so should not be used for more than a few days at a time.

Store essential oils out of reach of children.

Essential oils are flammable and so should be kept away from naked flames.

Candles and vaporizers must be kept out of reach of children and pets. Place them on heat-resistant surfaces and never leave them unattended. Metal candle holders become extremely hot with prolonged use.

Pregnant women should not use essential oils without seeking the advice of a doctor.

Do not perform an aromatherapy massage on someone who is unwell or who has torn muscles or broken bones.

essential oils

Essential oils have many therapeutic properties - some are relaxing, sedative and harmonizing; others are energizing, restorative and stimulating; many are soothing for the skin; some are thought to have an aphrodisiac action; and all of them have a profoundly uplifting effect on the emotions. However you choose to use them - individually or in blends; for bathing, massage, skincare and haircare; for vaporization or inhalation - the introduction of essential oils into your home spa bathing and beauty routine will enhance the pampering experience immeasurably.

Downshift from a busy week with essential oils that will help to restore your equilibrium. Stress has many causes and many symptoms, and professional aromatherapists will mix different blends of oils depending on the individual's personality and their stress levels. Stress-relieving essential oils are able to help calm a restless mind and counteract feelings of nervousness and apprehension. Many oils are recognized for their ability to deliver a sense of harmony and wellbeing. If you are feeling highly strung and over-emotional, they will help to ease anxiety and restore a sense of perspective, balance and objectivity. For the ultimate soothing experience, vaporize calming essential oils to create a tranquil environment while you soak in a comforting bath or enjoy a stress-relieving massage that will release any tension stored in your muscles.

Essential oils can also be used to help restore energy and vitality and improve concentration and creativity. On a physical level, they stimulate the circulation and revive heavy legs and aching muscles. On an emotional level, they will help to raise your spirits, increase alertness and counteract any feelings of lethargy. Keep a bottle of revitalizing oil, such as rosemary, with you and inhale a couple of drops from a tissue in emergencies.

basil

This soothing, awakening and uplifting oil should be used only in small quantities and not for prolonged periods of time or during pregnancy. Basil is a stimulating oil that can help to aid concentration and restore clarity of mind and enthusiasm. It can be used in the bath and for massage.

bergamot

Extracted from a fruit that resembles a miniature orange, bergamot oil is powerfully uplifting and can help to break the vicious cycle of stress and depression. Bergamot is a photosensitizer, increasing the skin's reaction to the sun and making it more likely to burn. For this reason, it should be used only in small amounts and not before exposure to the sun. Bergamot oil should be diluted in a carrier oil before being added to the bath and can also be used for massage.

camomile

German or Roman camomile oil is highly relaxing and sleep-inducing. It is also soothing to the skin and has the ability to protect it against ageing free radicals. Camomile oil is suitable for use in the bath, for massage and in haircare and skincare products.

cardamom

Cardamom is a restorative oil that is particularly helpful in alleviating fatigue and apathy. It is suitable for use in the bath and for massage.

clary sage

The Romans used clary sage as a universal remedy. It has soothing, restorative, mind-clearing properties and can be used in the bath, for massage and in haircare products. It should be avoided during pregnancy.

cypress

This revitalizing, astringent and decongestant oil is useful for easing painful periods and hot flushes. It is suitable for use in the bath, for massage and in skincare and haircare products. It should be avoided in the first three months of pregnancy.

eucalyptus

Used historically as an antiseptic and to protect against epidemics, eucalyptus oil is highly decongestant and a respiratory aid for colds; it is also healing and pain-relieving for cuts and wounds. It can be used in the bath, for massage and vaporization, and is also included in skincare and haircare products.

frankincense

A beautiful, restorative oil that is also very calming and relaxing, frankincense can also help to tone lined, slack skin and is often included in skincare preparations. The oil can be used in the bath, for massage and for vaporization.

geranium

Geranium is a relaxing oil that is widely used for its mood-lifting, antidepressant properties. It also relieves aching muscles and is helpful for alleviating premenstrual fluid retention. Geranium oil can be used in the bath, for massage, for vaporization, and in haircare and skincare preparations. However, you should avoid using it in high concentrations if you have sensitive skin.

grapefruit

Grapefruit oil can relieve nervous tension and relax the muscles. It is a cleansing, purifying oil that helps to aid detoxification. Grapefruit oil is a refreshing addition to baths and massage blends, but should not be used before exposure to the sun.

jasmine

Jasmine is a supremely soothing, antidepressant oil that can help to raise self-esteem and lift depression and pessimism. It is one of the most expensive oils because vast quantities of the petals are required to extract even a tiny amount of essential oil. However, it is a very powerful oil and can be used in very small quantities. Jasmine oil is an aphrodisiac and also has a soothing effect on muscular aches and tension. It should not be used during pregnancy and can irritate sensitive skin.

juniper

Juniper was used in incense by the ancient Romans and Greeks, who believed it helped deter evil spirits. It was also used as a disinfectant during epidemics. Juniper is a revitalizing oil that is a powerful detoxifier and diuretic. It is also antiseptic, astringent and healing, so is often highly effective in treating acne. It can be used in the bath, for vaporization and for skincare preparations. It should not be used during pregnancy and should be used only in very small quantities – less than 10 per cent of a blend. Spanish juniper is widely used in haircare products as it helps to control the production of sebum and is purifying for the scalp and hair.

lavender

The finest French lavender is grown high in the mountains of Provence – the best grows at an altitude of 1,000 metres. It is a highly antiseptic oil, which is very healing and soothing to the skin. It can be used in the bath, for massage, for vaporization, and in skincare and haircare products. Lavender oil is so gentle that it is the only essential oil that can be applied undiluted to the skin. It is a wonderful treatment for burns, bites and spots, as it helps to speed up healing and minimize blistering and scarring. Apply a drop of oil with a cotton bud to the affected area. Avoid using lavender oil during the first three months of pregnancy.

lavandin

This is a hybrid variety of blue and aspic lavender that is native to the Haute Provence region of France. It has a heady perfume that is reminiscent of camphor. Lavandin oil has similar relaxing properties to lavender. It is suitable for use in the bath but should be avoided during the first three months of pregnancy.

lemon

Lemon oil is astringent, healing, reviving and uplifting. It can be used in the bath, for massage, and in skincare and haircare products. Do not use lemon oil before exposure to the sun. It takes 3,000 lemons to produce just one kilo of essential oil.

lemongrass

This is a stimulating oil and a powerful tonic. Aromatherapist Patricia Davis recommends that it can be diluted in a carrier oil and rubbed into the temples to ease headaches. However, it should be used with care as it can cause skin irritation. For bathing, no more than 3 drops should be diluted in a carrier oil before being added to the bath water. Lemongrass oil has antiseptic and antibacterial properties and can be vaporized to purify the air; it is also a very effective, natural insect repellent.

lime

Lime is an uplifting, reviving and refreshing oil that can help to relieve anxiety and fatique. It should not be used before exposure to the sun. Lime oil acts as an antiseptic and has a stimulating effect on the circulation, so aiding detoxification.

mandarin

Mandarin oil gives a sensation of serenity. It can be used in the bath, for massage, and in skincare and haircare formulations, but not before exposure to the sun. It is the only essential oil that can be used on children.

marjoram

A warming and comforting oil, marjoram is often recommended by aromatherapists for use in steam inhalations as it can rapidly ease chest and respiratory problems. It is a strongly sedative oil and can be combined with lavender oil and used in the bath before bed to ease insomnia. Aromatherapist Gabriel Mojay advises using marjoram for those who are experiencing chronic lethargy or nervous exhaustion.

myrtle

Myrtle is an oil that is detoxifying to the tissues and is also a decongestant. It is suitable for use in the bath and in haircare products.

neroli

This beautifully scented, profoundly uplifting and calming oil is obtained from fresh orange blossom. It has antiseptic, regenerating properties and can be used in the bath, for massage, and in skincare and haircare products. It should not be used before exposure to the sun.

niaouli

Niaouli is an oil with healing and regenerating qualities, and is also a powerful antiseptic and anti-inflammatory. It is a very stimulating oil, so avoid using it late in the evening. Niaouli can be used in inhalations as it is a beneficial treatment for infections of the respiratory tract. It is also used in skincare preparations as it helps relieve oily skin, acne and fungal infections.

orange

As well as its calming, antidepressant properties, orange oil is recognized as a skin tonic and hair strengthener. It is suitable for use in the bath, for massage, and in skincare and haircare products. Do not use orange oil before exposure to the sun.

patchouli

An anti-inflammatory and antiseptic, patchouli oil is useful in treating a range of skin disorders, including acne, eczema and fungal infections such as athlete's foot. It is an antidepressant oil and can relieve feelings of anxiety. It will help to ground somebody who is stressed and will reduce a tendency to over-think. Patchouli is also considered to be an aphrodisiac.

peppermint

Harvested in Provence, peppermint oil is energizing, antiseptic, stimulating and pain-relieving. It can be used in small quantities (2–3 drops diluted in a carrier oil) in the bath, for massage, and in skincare and haircare preparations. It should be avoided during the first three months of pregnancy.

petitgrain

Petitgrain oil is distilled from the leaves of the bitter orange tree. It is an antidepressant and makes a refreshing bath oil. It is especially useful for soothing sensitive skin and can help to regulate the over-production of sebum in oily skin.

pine

Pine is an energizing oil that is also decongestant and toning. It is very effective at clearing the respiratory tract in the case of a cold and is suitable for use in inhalations, baths, for massage and vaporization. Pine oil is also used in haircare products.

rose and rosewood

Rose oil, which is extracted from the petals of the flower, is highly prized in anti-ageing skincare products and is especially good for dry skins. Roses have always been associated with love, and the oil is known for its aphrodisiac effect. It is also a relaxing oil that helps to relieve stress. Aromatherapists like rose oil for its ability to restore confidence. It is one of the most expensive oils because very large quantities of petals are needed to extract a small amount of essential oil. Rosewood is less expensive and not as potent as the flower-derived oil. Both of these oils can be used in the bath, for massage and for skincare.

rosemary

The ancient Greeks and Romans used rosemary in love potions and elixirs for long life. This stimulating, revitalizing and antiseptic oil is suitable for use in the bath, for massage, and in skincare and haircare products. It can also be used in inhalations or vaporization to help clear the mind and aid concentration and memory. Do not use this oil during pregnancy or if you suffer from epilepsy or high blood pressure.

sandalwood

Sandalwood is a balancing oil that has antiseptic qualities and is effective in massage and inhalations, especially for dry coughs and sore throats. It can also be used in the bath. Sandalwood is an aphrodisiac, often used in perfumery. Avoid West Indian and Australian sandalwood, neither of which have therapeutic value.

tea tree

Used for centuries by the Australian Aborigines to clean wounds, tea tree oil (also known as Melaleuca oil) is antibacterial, antiviral, antifungal, and invigorating. It is suitable for use in the bath and is a valuable oil for treating skin problems, especially acne, and is often included in haircare preparations as it can help control dandruff. Tea tree oil helps to develop a positive mental outlook and can build confidence.

ylang ylang

Ylang ylang is a relaxing oil that procures a deep sense of wellbeing and is also toning to the skin. It is suitable for use in the bath, for massage, and in skincare and haircare products.

aromatherapy blends

Calming Vaporization Blend

Place the following oils in a little warm water in the well of your vaporizer and then light the candle or plug it in. Or, drop the oils into a small bowl of water and place it on a radiator:

2 drops ylang ylang essential oil
2 drops orange essential oil

Romantic Bath Blend

To 20 ml (one tablespoon) of carrier oil or foam bath add:

2 drops rose essential oil
2 drops ylang ylang essential oil
2 drops lemon essential oil

Stress-Relieving Bath Blend

To 20 ml (one tablespoon) of carrier oil or foam bath add:

2 drops geranium essential oil
2 drops lavender or lavandin essential oil
1 drop rosewood essential oil

Luxurious Bath Blend

To 20 ml (one tablespoon) of carrier oil or foam bath add:

3 drops rose essential oil
2 drops sandalwood essential oil
1 drop juniper essential oil

Reviving Leg Lotion

Use this reviving leg lotion during hot weather, after a long flight or if you are suffering from fluid retention.

To 10 ml of a neutral body lotion add:

2 drops lemon essential oil
2 drops cypress essential oil
1 drop sandalwood essential oil

Energizing Massage Blend

To 30 ml of sweet almond oil add:

4 drops grapefruit essential oil
4 drops lime essential oil
2 drops rosemary essential oil

Soothing Massage Blend

To 30 ml of sweet almond oil add:

4 drops petitgrain essential oil
3 drops camomile essential oil
3 drops jasmine essential oil

Calming Massage Blend

To 30 ml of sweet almond oil add:

4 drops sandalwood essential oil
4 drops patchouli essential oil
2 drops basil essential oil

Decongestant Inhalation

This blend is highly decongestant and will help to clear the respiratory tract if you are suffering from a cold.

1 drop pine essential oil
1 drop eucalyptus essential oil
1 drop peppermint essential oil

Relaxing Inhalation

This blend will help calm you if you are suffering from anxiety:

3 drops orange essential oil
2 drops lavender essential oil
2 drops marjoram essential oil

Put the oils in a bowl of steaming water and place a towel over your head so that it covers the bowl entirely. Do not do an inhalation if you suffer from asthma, hay fever or an allergy.

L'Occitane Headquarters

L'OCCITANE
BP307
04103 Manosque Cedex
France
Tel: 00 33 4 92 70 19 00
Fax: 00 33 4 92 87 34 23
Toll free: 0800 20 11 46
accueil@loccitane.fr
http://www.loccitane.fr

L'OCCITANE LIMITED
237 Regent St
London W1R 7AG
England
Tel: 00 44 207 290 1420
Fax: 00 44 207 290 1429
Mail Order:
00 44 207 209 1421
mailorder@loccitane.co.uk
http://www.loccitane.net

L'OCCITANE INC.
10 East 39th St, 8th Floor
New York, NY 10016
USA
Tel: 1 212 696 9098
Fax: 1 212 213 0803
customer.service@loccitane.net
Toll free: 1 888 623 2880
http://www.loccitane.com

L'OCCITANE AUTRICHE GESMBH
Panoramaweg 35
A-9500 Villach
Austria
Tel: 00 43 424 251 222
Fax: 00 43 424 251 2224
occitane.hajek@aon.at

L'OCCITANE FAR EAST
2403 Universal Trade Centre
3 Arbuthnot Rd Central
Hong Kong
Tel: 00 852 2 868 0778
Fax: 00 852 2 845 0159
occitane@hkstar.com

L'OCCITANE DO BRAZIL
Rua Normandia 18
São Paulo SP 04517-040
Brazil
Tel: 00 55 11 530 8656
Fax: 00 55 11 530 8656
geral@loccitane.com.br
Toll free: 0800 171 272

L'Occitane Stores

AFRICA

MOROCCO
Casablanca
1 Bd Abdellatif Ben Kaddour

TUNISIA
Tunis
Les Berges du Lac

AMERICA

ARGENTINA
Buenos Aires
Calle Uruguay 1137

BRAZIL
São Paulo
Morumbi Shopping, Loja 90 S
Shopping Jardim Sul, Loja 222A
Shopping Patio Higienopolis, Loja 240
Rua Normandia, 18 Moema
Curutiba
Shopping Crystal Plaza, Loja 232
Rio de Janeiro
Barra Shopping, Loja 131 C

CANADA
Vancouver BC
3051 Granville St

MEXICO
Mazatlan
Av. Camaron Sabalo 109

LA REUNION
Saint Denis
20 bis, rue Félix Guyon

SAINT MARTIN ISLAND
Marigot
Marina Center

UNITED STATES
New York, NY
Madision Ave at 80th St
Madision Ave at 52nd St
Columbus Ave at 69th St
Spring St at Wooster St
Grand Central Station
Huntington, NY
Walt Whitman Mall
White Plains, NY
The Westchester Mall
Beverly Hills, CA
Beverly Drive
San Diego, CA
Fashion Valley Shopping Center
Sacramento, CA
Arden Fair
Glendale, CA
Glendale Galleria
Los Angeles, CA
Century City
Farmington, CT
The Westfarms Mall
Washington, DC
M St NW
Miami, FL
Dadeland Mall
Boca Raton, FL
Boca Town Center
Chicago, IL
900 North Michigan
Chicago, IL
Lincoln Park
Skokle, IL
Old Orchard Center
Oak Brook, IL
Oakbrook Center
Baintree, MA
South Shore Plaza
Troy, MI
Somerset Collection
Short Hills, NJ
The Mall at Short Hills
Paramus, NJ
Garden State Plaza
Portland, OR
Pioneer Place
McClean, VA
Tyson's Corner
Arlington, VA
Fashion Center, Pentagon City
Norfolk, VA
MacArthur Center
Seattle, WA
Pacific Place

ASIA

HONG KONG
Hong Kong
The Landmark Central, Shop B62
Style House, Park Lane Hotel, Causeway Bay
Kowloon
Festival Walk, Shop UG15, Kowloon Tong

JAPAN
Toyko
6-9-5 Ginza Konatsu, Chuo-ku
3-5-18 Kita Aoyama Minato-ku
Yokohama
Landmark Tower, 2-3-2 Minato Mirai Nishi Ku

KOREA
Seoul
Apkujeong Shop, Kangnam-Ku
Sungnam
Samsung Plaza, DunDang-Ku

PHILIPINES
Makati City
Rustan's Dept. Store, Ayala Ave

SINGAPORE
Singapore
Takashimaya Shopping Center, 391 Orchard Rd

TAIWAN
Taipei
Ta-An Shop, N° 140/1F Ta-An Rd, Sec 1
Taichung City
Taichung Shop, N°62/1F Chin Min Yi St
Tainan City
Mitsukoshi Tainan, N°162/4F Chun Shan Rd
Kaohsiung City
Mitsukoshi Kaohsiung, N°213/4F San Do San Rd

AUSTRALASIA

AUSTRALIA
Noosa Heads
Hastings St, Shop 4 French Quarter Resort
Melbourne
70 Church, Brighton

NEW ZEALAND
Auckland
274 Broadway – Newmarket

EUROPE

AUSTRIA
Graz
Schmiedgasse 21
Vienna
Seilergasse 1

BELGIUM
Anvers
Wijnegem Shopping Center, Turnhoutsebaan 5

CYPRUS
Nicosia
Boumboulinas St, 17

FRANCE
Paris
1er – 1 rue du 29 Julliet
1er – Carrousel du Louvre
4e – 84 rue de Rivoli
4e – 17 rue des Francs Bourgeois
4e – 55 rue St-Louis-en L'Isle
4e – 18 Place des Vosges
5e – 130 rue Mouffetard

6e – 26 rue Vavin
6e – 95 rue de Rennes
7e – 90 rue du Bac
8e – 84 Av. Champs-Elysées
9e – Passage du Havre
109 rue Saint Lazare
15e – 27 rue du Commerce
16e – 12 rue d'Auteuil
16e – 109 Av. Victor Hugo
16e – 53 rue de Passy

Région Parisienne
78 Le Chesnay – Centre Commercial Parly 2
78 St-Germain-en-Laye – 3 rue des Louviers
78 Versailles – 7 rue Ducis
78 Mantes-la-Jolie – 32, rue des Thiers
92 Levallois – 32 rue Louise Michel
92 Boulogne-Billancourt – 93 Bd Jean Jaurès
94 Nogent sur Marne – 122 Grand rue Charles de Gaulle

Amboise
21 rue Nationale

Besançon
3 Grande rue

Cannes
14 rue du Marechal Joffre

Cambrai
19 rue des Rôtisseurs

Clermont Ferrand
38 bis, rue des Gras

Colmar
18 rue des Marchands

Dijon
22 rue Piron

Epinal
16 rue des Minimes

La Rochelle
6 rue Chaudrier

Le Puy
70 rue Chaussade

Lille
19 rue Neuve

Lyon
2e – 5 rue Victor Hugo
5e – 4 bis, rue Saint-Jean

Manosque
21 rue Grande

Montpellier
26 grand rue Jean Moulin

Nantes
Passage Pommeraye

Nancy
14 rue Gambetta

Orléans
5 rue Charles Sanglier

Reims
25 Passage Talleyrand

Rennes
1 rue de la Motte Fablet

St Etienne
7 rue Michelet

Strasbourg
90 Grand Rue

Thionville
Centre Commercial Geric

Toulouse
9 rue du Lieutenant Colonel Pelissier

Tours
8 rue de Bordeaux

Troyes
38 rue Emile Zola

Valenciennes
Avenue d'Amsterdam

Volx
Les Fours à Chaux

GERMANY

Hamburg
Mönckebergstrasse 7, Levantehaus

GREECE

Athens
Patriarchou Loakeim 1- Kolonaki

IRELAND

Dublin
15 Wicklow St

LUXEMBOURG

Luxembourg
7 Grand Rue

PORTUGAL

Lisbon
Av. S. Joao de Deus 41 G (Av. Di Roma)

SPAIN

Barcelona
Rambla de Cataluna, 61

Madrid
C/Velazquez 45

Marbella
Av. Ricardo Soriano 45 Local 6

SWITZERLAND

Lausanne
Petit Chêne 1-3, 1003

UK

London
237 Regent St
70 Kensington High St
67 Kings Rd

Greenhithe
Lower Guild Hall, Bluewater, Kent

MIDDLE EAST

ISRAEL

Tel Aviv
Dizengof Center – Gate 6
Kikar Hamedina, 72 Hey-be'eyar St

Ramat Hashron
55 Sokolove St

Rahanana
Renanim Mall, 2 Hamelacha St

LEBANON

Beirut
Av. Du Président Elias Sarkis Immeuble Archar, Archrafieh

UAE

Dubai
Shopping Center at Twin Tower

Sharjah
Al Taawun Center

Complementary Therapies

Aromatherapy Associates Ltd
68 Maltings Place, Bagleys Lane, London SW6 2BY
Tel: 020 7371 9878

Aromatherapy Organizations Council
Contact for information, and training facilities and practitioners in your area: PO Box 355, Croydon, Surrey CR9 2QP

International Society of Professional Aromatherapists
ISPA House, 82 Ashby Rd, Hinckley, Leicestershire LE10 1SN

Aromatherapy Trade Council
PO Box 52, Market Harborough, Leicestershire LE16 8ZX
Tel: 01858 434 242

Bach Flower Remedies
Bach Foundation, Mount Vernon, Sotwell, Wallingford Oxfordshire OX10 0PZ

British Massage Therapy Council
Greenbank House, 65a Adelphi St, Preston PR1 7BH
Tel: 01772 881063

The British Wheel of Yoga
1 Hamilton Place, Boston Rd, Sleaford, Lincolnshire NG34 7ES
Tel: 01529 306851

General Council & Register of Consultant Herbalists
Grosvenor House, 40 Sea Way, Middleton-on-Sea, West Sussex PO22 7BA

International Stress Management
Association (UK), Southbank University, LPSS, 103 Borough Rd, London SE1 0AA

Larkhall Swiss Laboratories
Hair sample testing to determine mineral status.
Tel: 020 8874 1130

Society of Homoeopaths
2 Artizan Rd, Northampton NN1 4HU
Tel: 01604 21400

Mail Order for Home Spa Products

Harrods Ltd
Grant Way, off Syon Lane, Isleworth, Middlesex TW7 5QD
Credit card phone line: 0800 730123
Or contact the store: 87–135 Brompton Rd, Knightsbridge, London SW1X 7RJ
Tel: 020 7730 1234

Harvey Nichols
109–125 Knightsbridge London SWIX 7RJ
Tel: 020 7235 5000

Liberty Mail Order Dept.
Regent St, London W1R 6AH
Tel: 020 7734 1234

Selfridges
400 Oxford St, London W1A 1AB
Tel: 020 7629 1234

Space NK
41 Earlham St, London WC2H 9LD
Tel: 020 7636 2523

Figures in bold indicate main references.

With special thanks to Venetia Penfold of Carlton Books for conceiving the Home Spa concept, to Zia Mattocks for editing it with such attention to detail and for her beautiful use of language, and to Barbara Zuñiga for her brilliant art direction and luscious, contemporary design.

A big thank you to Graham Atkins-Hughes for the evocative photography and to Emily Jewsbury for her talented styling.

Inspiration was provided by L'Occitane en Provence's exquisite product ranges, and the author would like to extend her thanks to Kit Braden and Malika Browne for their support.

Aromatherapist and crystal healer Gita Jobanputra of 140 Harley St, London, England (020 7487 5873), kindly contributed the *Home Spa* aromatherapy recipes, and Aromatherapy Associates, London, offered their expert help in checking them.

I am also indebted for their support to Emily, Russ, Jill and Anthony Malkin, Jenny and Tom Bull, Ashley Hobday, Alison Campbell and to the team at Colman Getty Public Relations.

Quotes were derived from the following sources:

p. 13. Housden, Roger, *Soul and Sensuality: Returning the Erotic to Everyday Life*, London, Rider (an imprint of Random House), 1993

p. 42. Daudet, Alphonse, *Letters from my Mill and Letters to an Absent One*, Ayer Co Publishing, 1971

p. 61. Kingsley, Philip, *The Complete Hair Book: The Ultimate Guide to your Hair's Health and Beauty*, New York, Grove Press, Inc., 1979

p. 73. Antoine-Dariaux, Geneviève, *Elegance: A Complete Guide for Every Woman who wants to be Well and Properly Dressed on all Occasions*, Great Britain, Frederick Muller Limited, 1964

p. 93. Valery, Marie-Françoise, *Gardens of Provence and Côte d'Azur*, Germany, Taschen, 1998

p. 94. Trueman, John, *The Romantic Story of Scent*, London, Aldus Books, 1975

p. 97. Suskind, Patrick, translated by Woods, John E, *Perfume: the Story of a Murderer*, Harmondsworth, Penguin, 1986

pp. 125 and 127. Worwood, Valerie Ann, *The Fragrant Pharmacy*, London Macmillan, 1990

Bibliography

Alexander, Jane, *Spirit of the Home*, London, Thorsons, 1998

de Bonneville, Françoise, *The Book of the Bath* (English translation), London, Thames and Hudson Ltd, 1998

Davis, Patricia, *Aromatherapy an A–Z*, Saffron Walden, C W Daniel Company Limited, 1988

Edwards, Michael, *Perfume Legends – French Feminine Fragrances*, France, Michael Edwards & Co Pty Ltd in association with HM Editions, 1996

Irvine, Susan, *Perfume – The Creation and Allure of Classic Fragrances*, London, Haldane Mason Ltd (distributed by Aurum Press, London), 1996

Jones North, Jacquelyne Y, *Perfume, Cologne and Scent Bottles*, West Chester, Pennsylvania, Schiffer Publishing Ltd, 1986

Marsh, Madeleine, *Miller's Perfume Bottles – A Collector's Guide*, London, Mitchell Beazley, 1999

Mojay, Gabriel, *Aromatherapy for Healing the Spirit*, London, Gaia Books Limited, 1996

Oakes, John, *The Book of Perfumes*, London, Prion, 1998

Pallingston, Jessica, *Lipstick*, USA, St Martin's Press, 1999

Rimmel, Eugene, *The Book of Perfumes*, London, Chapman and Hall, 1865

The publishers would like to thank the following sources for their kind permission to reproduce the pictures in this book:
All photography by Graham Atkins-Hughes copyright of Carlton Books Limited apart from:
Graeme Montgomery/Art direction: Egan Melia Limited, London 20, 23, 47, 70/1, 78, 80, 82, 83, 85, 103
Every effort has been made to acknowledge correctly and contact the source and/copyright holder of each picture, and Carlton Books Limited apologizes for any unintentional errors or omissions which will be corrected in future editions of this book.